ICELAND

LANDMANNALAUGAR
hiking & trekking

SMART TRAVEL GUIDE

for nature lovers,
hikers, trekkers,
photographers

2019

"ICELAND: LANDMANNALAUGAR, hiking & trekking" – a smart travel guide for nature lovers, hikers, trekkers, photographers, -wilderness explorer series-, 1st edition, by Oleg Senkov

Copyright © 2019 by Oleg Senkov

Disclaimer. Although, I was trying to make every effort to be as accurate, precise and up-to-date as possible with all information I researched and present here, in this travel guide book, some unavoidable imprecisions may occur, due to the fast pace of ever-changing world. Thus, I disclaim myself from any liability to any party to any loss, damage or disruption during your travel and using the book as a source of information.

ABOUT AUTHOR AND THE BOOK

Oleg Senkov, PhD

I am a biologist, wildlife and travel photographer, writer, journalist and explorer, living in Germany. Over the last ~10 years I have published dozens of articles about nature, science, wildlife and travel in "**National Geographic**", "**National Geographic Traveler**", "**GEO**" and "**Scientific American**" magazines. Besides that, for the last ~25 years, I have conducted myself many research projects and published numerous scientific papers, reviews and book chapters in the field of neuroscience, learning and memory, and behavior of animals. This is my 5th travel guide book, and the second about the land of "*ice and fire*" – ICELAND (first 3 books were about wonderful **PATAGONIA: Peninsula Valdes** Nature Reserve; **Torres del Paine** National Park; **Tierra del Fuego** Land, see all my books, *Kindle* and *paperback* formats at my **AMAZON**'s Author Page: (www.amazon.com/author/olegsenkov), which I decided to write after I was so much impressed by **Patagonia**, during my trip to this fascinating "end-of-the-world" wilderness in Spring, 2017. I only regret that I was missing in this trip such "smart" travel guide, otherwise, I would be much more efficient as a wildlife photographer and traveler. With this 5th book, I continue my "*wilderness explorer series*", and describe here *Landmannalaugar*, colorful rainbow-like mountains in ICELAND, *Fjallabak* **Nature Reserve,** hiking and trekking trails in full detail, after I made 2 different expeditions through this remote and highly volcanic region in the rough-yet-beautiful close-to Arctic Circle land - ICELAND. I hope the book will be a good "practical tool", an all-to-know set of guidebooks for you (for me as well), while you are exploring the world with responsible mind and open heart as a truly nature lover.

My social media, travel and photography websites.
www.olegsenkov.com
www.facebook.com/oleg.senkov

MY BOOKS

You can buy my digital format *Kindle* books from *"Wilderness Explorer Series"* at any **13 Amazon's** webstores around the world, and the paperback books at **7 Amazon** webstores and some other third-parties bookshops; I will give you a link to my Amazon.com **author's page**, where you'll find all my books in different formats, book descriptions, photos and more:

my **AMAZON**'s **Author Page**: www.amazon.com/author/olegsenkov

From there, you can allocate my books at your national Amazon's webstore by coping and pasting a book title or my name into the Amazon's product search line. If your country does not have yet an Amazon's webstore, you can buy digital book formats, like *Kindle*, at any online store from 13 Amazon's stores, you just need an Amazon's account, e.g. there are not yet stores in Argentina and Chile, but you can buy digital *Kindle* books at the Spanish Amazon (www.amazon.es), or Brazilian (www.amazon.com.br). Alternatively, you can buy digital books directly from your **Kindle App** or **Kindle reader**. However, if you want to buy paperback books, they require delivery, so, choose the closest country, where you can buy them to minimize delivery costs; remember that the Amazon's webstore interface language as well as a purchase country you can always switch back and forth at the bottom of Amazon's webpage. For example, if you are in Norway, where're no yet any Amazon stores, you can order paperback books from the closest to you country, Germany, where's Amazon, switching webstore's interface language to English, if you do not know German.

wilderness explorer series

Oleg Senkov

ICELAND

waterfalls, volcanoes, glaciers, canyons,
hot springs, lakes, geysers, craters, lava fields

ICELAND

260 GPS coordinates
49 sights with **49** images
40 campsites + hiking trails
prices in ISK, €
90 websites
how to get info + buses
OSMAND map linked

for:
landscape photographers
hikers & trekkers
nature lovers
adventure seekers
budget travelers

SMART TRAVEL GUIDE

"ICELAND: waterfalls, volcanoes, glaciers, canyons, hot springs, lakes, geysers, craters, lava fields" is my 4th travel guide book in the "wilderness explorer" series, and 2nd about ICELAND, see my Amazon's Author Page www.amazon.com/author/olegsenkov.

This "smart" travel guide contains ~**260 GPS** coordinates of important to know places in ICELAND, ~**90 website links**, covering: best viewpoints, ~**40 campsites** with detailed info and prices, **hiking trails** around, The book first describes how to get to ICELAND with a ferry from Denmark or by air, then, how to commute within ICELAND with a bus, a rented car or hitchhiking, after that I give the most important advices how to survive as adventurous hiker, how to safely do **multiday trekking** in **dangerous Highlands**, and then finally, I review in detail **49 different key sights** around ICELAND with **49 images**: these are **17 waterfalls**, **11 volcanoes**, **4 mounts/rocks**, **4 geothermal areas and geysers**, **7 lakes/lagoons**, and **6 cracks/canyons**. The book can be equally useful for "**budget**" adventure seekers, solo/group travelers, in "fast & easy" style with a rented car/campers or travel agency users as well as for paid **wildlife** and **travel/landscape photographers** on a mission. I hope the book will be a good "practical tool", an all-to-know set of guidebooks for you (for me as well), while you are exploring the world with responsible mind and open heart as a truly nature lover.

wilderness explorer series

Oleg Senkov

PATAGONIA
Tierra del Fuego

245 GPS coordinates
20 images
17 hiking trails
2 trekking maps
prices in AR$, US$, €
70 website links
hiking trails elevations

for:
wildlife photographers
hikers & trekkers
nature lovers
budget travelers

SMART TRAVEL GUIDE

"*Patagonia: Tierra del Fuego*" is my 3rd book in the "*wilderness explorer*" series (the first one I wrote about Peninsula Valdes, the second – about Torres del Paine National Park, which I hope, will be a good "practical tool", an all-to-know set of guide books for you (for me as well), while you are exploring the world with responsible mind and open heart as a truly nature lover. The book contains **~245 GPS coordinates** of important to know places, **~70 website links**, covering all the important **campsites**, hotels, viewpoints, trails, key sightseeing, it has **2 detailed trekking maps**, and **~20 photographs** I made in March-April 2017. The book first describes how to get in/out the "Tierra del Fuego" park and Ushuaia, all park's updated **rules and prices**, then I in very detail describe **17 different hikes** in the park and around, including hikes: to **Martial Glacier**, **Esmeralda Lagoon**, **Lago Roca**, **Guanaco trail**, **Pampa Alta**, **Laguna del Cominante**, **Waterfall Los Amigos**, **Mount Cortez**, multiday trekking in **Sierra Valdivieso Circuit**, long **Beagle Channel Trail**, and finally, **Southernmost multiday trekking Dientes de Navarino**. I also give all the details for wild and paid camping, hostels, food stores, roads conditions, travel scenarios, public buses, prices for touristic services, paid tours, wildlife safaris, fishing, kayaking, At the end of the guide, I give detailed information what kind of wild animals and where you can meet in Tierra del Fuego land (**Magellanic penguins**, **Gentoo penguins**, **King penguins**, condors, huemul, guanaco, fox, **sea lions**, **beavers**) and their behavior. The book can be equally useful for "budget" adventure seekers, solo/group travelers, "fast & easy" with a rented car/campers or travel agency users as well as for paid wildlife and travel/landscape photographers on a mission.

wilderness explorer series

Oleg Senkov

PATAGONIA
Torres del Paine
National Park

90 GPS coordinates
14 images
1 trekking map
prices in AR$, US$, €
40 website links
hiking trails elevations

for:
wildlife photographers
hikers & trekkers
nature lovers
budget travelers

SMART TRAVEL GUIDE

"**Patagonia: Torres del Paine National Park**" is my **second book** in the "*wilderness explorer*" series (first one I wrote about Peninsula Valdes, which I hope, will be a good "**practical tool**", an all-to-know set of guide books for you (for me as well), while you are exploring the world with responsible mind and open heart as a truly nature lover. The book contains **~90 GPS** coordinates of important to know places, **~40 website links**, covering all the important campsites, hotels, viewpoints, trails, key sightseeing, it has a detailed **trekking map**, and **~14 photographs** I made in March-April 2017. The book first describes how to get in/out the park, all park's **updated rules and prices**, then how to design your trekking route and how to book all accommodation in the park and nearby. In addition to popular "**W**" and "**O**" trekking circuits in the park, I give information about another **6 less-known, secret "off-the-bitten-pass" trails**. I also give all the details for wild and paid camping, hotels, hostels, domes, cabins, food stores, roads conditions, travel scenarios, public buses, prices for touristic services, paid tours, wildlife safaris, fishing, kayaking, horseback riding. At the end of the guide, I give detailed information what kind of **wild animals** and where you can meet in the park (**puma**, **condors**, huemul, guanaco, fox) and their behavior. I also describe where you can find fossils from **Jurassic Era of ichthyosaur**, of a large prehistoric marine dolphin-like predator, or to see **ancient cave** paintings of indigenous tribes lived here 3,000-8,000 years ago. The book can be equally useful for "budget" adventure seekers, solo/group travelers, "fast & easy" with a rented car/campers or travel agency users as well as for paid wildlife and travel photographers on a mission

wilderness explorer series

Oleg Senkov

PATAGONIA
Peninsula Valdés

60 GPS coordinates
20 images
1 wildlife map
prices in AR$, US$, €
35 website links

for:
wildlife photographers
hikers & trekkers
nature lovers
budget travelers

SMART TRAVEL GUIDE

"**Patagonia: Peninsula Valdés**" is a unique "smart" travel guide, which I made at first to be solely used in my own, after buying so many travel guides and still feeling - they aren't good enough for my adventures to explore wilderness as a biologist and wildlife photographer. I was missing it during my trip to Patagonia in 2017, otherwise, I would be much more efficient as a wildlife photographer and traveler. With this first book, I start my new "wilderness explorer series", which I hope, will be a good "practical tool", an all-to-know set of guide books for you (for me as well), while you are exploring the world with responsible mind and open heart as a truly nature lover. The book contains **~60 GPS** coordinates of important to know places, **~35 website links**, covering about 20 different the most spectacular sightseeing locations at the Peninsular Valdes and around, it has a detailed **wildlife map**, and over **20 photographs** I made in March-April 2017. The book describes all **specific photographic seasons** when wild animals can be sighted: e.g. when orcas, **killer whales**, can beach themselves in order to catch sea lion pups, or when is the best to see **Magellanic penguins** or **fighting "beachmasters"** of gigantic **Elephant seals** with intruder male seals, or when and where is the best to be to witness **Southern Right whales** coming very close to shores with their calves vocalizing and breaching out of peninsula's waters. I also give all the information for wild and paid **camping**, hotels and **hostels**, supermarkets, gasoline stations and ATMs, roads conditions, travel scenarios, airports, **public buses**, prices for certain touristic services, wildlife safaris, **whale watching**. There is a very detailed and updated chapter for travel means with long-distance buses and flights in Patagonia and Argentina, including **how to get in/out in Buenos Aires** airports, a main bus station, and a train station. The book can be equally useful for "budget" adventure seekers, "fast & easy" with a rented car or travel agency travelers as well as for paid wildlife and travel photographers on a mission.

HOW TO USE GPS COORDINATES

"OSMAND", "OSMAND+" "GOOGLE MAP", and "MAPS.ME"

In the *Kindle* format of my books, it is very practical and easy to use **GPS locations** of any key landmarks, trails, routes, viewpoints, shops, campsites, banks, hostels… etc. I give in the book GPS decimal coordinates as links [🌐 64.787470, -18.421448], once you click at the link, it will be automatically opened in "**OsmAnd**" or "**OsmAnd+**" **App** (www.osmand.net) in your mobile gadget (smartphone, tablet), showing the location *just in the middle of your screen*. "**OsmAnd+**" is an open-source subscription-based (~€1.5/Month) off-line travel map ("**OsmAnd**" is free) navigation and GPS recorder, based on OpenStreetMap data (www.openstreetmap.org) and "**Wikipedia**" for **hikers**, **trekkers**, **cyclists**, **drivers**, who wish to have a very detailed constantly updated (40,000+ contributors) topographic map with hill-shade contour lines, all marked trails, routes, roads, forests, national parks, natural reserves, cities, POI, public transport and more… While "**OsmAnd**" is totally free, you can download it from "**Google Play**", "**App Store**" or "**Amazons Apps**", however, if you wish, you still can use book's GPS coordinates in other navigation Apps like "**Google Map**" App, or "**MAPS.ME**" App, by coping and pasting the sequence of digits as coordinates 64.787470, -18.421448 from the book into the search line in your navigation App. To use any of mentioned above navigation Apps for ICELAND, you must download maps for ICELAND. "**Google Map**" App has also such a function like "**offline maps**", simply, go in "settings", select "offline maps", click at "select your own map", then locate on screen a map you want to download and make available offline, and download it. However, if you use a paperback format of my guidebooks, to use GPS coordinates from the books, you have to type them manually into your navigation App, so, they still can be usable, although, less convenient.

Contents

ICELAND

ABOUT ICELAND

Iceland – is a rather huge island-country (103,000 km², 18th world place by island size), located at the North portion of the Atlantic Ocean [🌍 64.787470, -18.421448], ~1000 km from Norway, ~450 km from Faroe Islands, ~900 km from UK, ~1500 km from Denmark, ~2200 km from Canada, and only ~300 km from Greenland. It is sitting right on the **Mid-Atlantic Ridge** (this is why it has so many active volcanoes, ~32, and total number >130), where the North American and Eurasian tectonic plates drift from each other with speed about 2 cm/year. Therefore, everything is moving here, changing, boiling, steaming, shaking... If you would like to see an outdoor gigantic performance of how the Earth has been forming for millions and millions of years in the past, - come here, it is a land of myriad of different landscapes, matter forms, glaciers, deep canyons, enormous waterfalls, endless covered-with-1000-years-old moss lava fields, cone-like reddish craters, turquoise iceberg lagoons, furious glacial rivers, hot bathing springs, tall geysers, colorful rainbow-like mountains, soil steamers, standing like gigantic trolls rock pillars, volcanic black sand beaches, fairytale caves - a truly **land of ice and fire**! It has population ~358,780 people (~2/3 live in the capital

Reykjavik [🌍 64.123514, -21.881323]), who produced Growth Domestic Product (**GDP**) in 2018 ~$27 billion, with one of the highest in the world (**5th place**) GDP per person, $GDP_{2018/capita}$ ~ $75,700. It is located just below the **Arctic Circle** (latitude: 66° 33' 39" N or 66.56083°); its Northernmost small island ~40

km from mainland's shore called *Grimsey* [🌍 66.539967, -18.013410] (size ~5.3 km², population ~60 people and 10,000+ puffins) has an official stand of the Arctic Circle and any tourists who sail there, can receive a certificate of crossing the Polar Circle. However, the climate at Iceland is warmer than one can expect, considering so close location to the Arctic region; in average in Winter, it is about -5° to +3° C, and in Summer, it is +8° to +15° C, and it's because the Icelandic climate is so much influenced by a very close proximity to the warm **Gulf Stream** (~100 km wide, ~1 km thickness of water flow layer, it flows around Iceland at its Eastern,-Westernmost shores).

FACTS ABOUT ICELAND

There are plenty of interesting and inspiring facts about Iceland and Icelanders, which you can find in many travel guides and in Internet; I will list here just a few to ignite your curiosity, not to pre-condition your perception of this beautiful island of *"ice and fire"* before your travel, - you should make your own discoveries about the country and people living there.

Worth to know (practical) facts:

1) Iceland has no mosquitoes, no bears, no snakes... - no dangerous animals, however, you have to know that there are a few types of flies, which can be very annoyíng in wet lowlands, around lakes, plus, there were cases when polar bears from nearby Greenland visited Iceland in cold Winters, wandering through on frozen sea ice shield, so, your chances to see polar bear in Iceland aren't entirely zero;

2) Iceland has one of the lowest **crime rates** in the world: **rate 0.3** (intentional homicide victims per 100,000 inhabitants), to compare: Switzerland (0.54), New Zealand/Australia (0.99), Germany (1.18), United Kingdom (1.2), United States (5.35), Russia (10.82), Brazil (29.53), Venezuela (56.33). Hereby, it must be very safe to travel through Iceland, however, you have to consider a fact that according to the Icelandic Tourist Board, a total of **2,195,271 tourists** visited Iceland in 2017, it is around 6 times more than the whole population of Iceland, and people tend to behave in similar way or slightly better (as guests) as in their home countries, with 1:1 ethical, moral and cultural standards, so, having that said, to conclude, be rational, not pre-conditioned, Iceland in general is very safe, but bad things may happen too, thus, taking care about your own safety as you would do back home or in any other European country – is a good strategy;

3) You can sight **Northern Lights** in Iceland not only in Winter, but even in late Summer or Autumn; to witness the Aurora Borealis you need clouds-free dark night sky (no artificial light pollution around), some solar storms on the Sun with coming to the Earth solar winds carrying charged particles and be somewhere in Northern regions of Iceland (e.g. *Mývatn*, *Akureyri*, *Húsavík*); in Winter you can see Auroras even in *Reykjavik*; to make your chances to see the **Aurora Borealis** higher, use official Icelandic forecast for Northern Lights with online updated 24/7 maps (https://en.vedur.is/weather/forecasts/aurora), plus, a forecast for clouds (https://en.vedur.is/weather/forecasts/cloudcover).

4) Despite the International Whaling Commission's Ban on commercial whaling since 1986, and in contrary to the fact that there are no real large economic benefits (according to the University of Iceland's report, whale watching contributed $13.4 million to the economy, while the whale hunting company Hval hf. contributed only $8.4 million), Iceland sadly continues to kill *minke* and *fin* whales as its government has announced recently new quotes: it will be allowed up to **2,000 whales** to be killed in the next five years. The fact is that vast majority of Icelanders nowadays do not support whale hunting, you can see in all local newspapers and

media slogans like: "I am pure Icelander, I do not eat whale meat", yet, killing of these magnificent and intellectual marine mammals continues, although with a lesser pace, and the reason is because whale meat is sold mostly to tourists in Icelandic restaurants and some exported to Japan. Thus, if you love nature and wildlife, and would like to contribute for protection of these great animals, please, **refuse from eating whale meat** in Iceland, and elsewhere, instead, take a **whale watching tour** (*Reykjavik*, *Akureyri*, *Húsavík*) to support local communities economically, and to enjoy yourself enormously by meeting in person these marine giants!!!

USEFUL LINKS

www.iceland.is – official main gateway to Iceland

www.visiticeland.com – official Icelandic travel guide

www.road.is – information about conditions in **all roads** over the whole Iceland

www.vedur.is – main Icelandic **Meteorological Office**, which provides forecasts for weather (wind, temperature, precipitation), earthquakes, floods, avalanches, volcanic air pollution, radiation 24/7 for a week ahead for the entire Iceland

www.safetravel.is – **personal safety**, weather and road conditions, you can submit your hiking/trekking route for safety reason

www.south.is – visit **South Iceland**, official travel guide for South Iceland

www.northiceland.is – visit **North Iceland**, official Travel Guide to North Iceland

www.east.is - visit **East Iceland**, official travel guide for East Iceland

www.west.is - visit **West Iceland**, official travel guide for West Iceland

www.visitreykjanes.is – visit Reykjanes, official travel guide to Reykjanes Iceland

www.guidetoiceland.is – a very good and detailed guide for Iceland, region by region

HOW TO GET HERE

You can get to Iceland by two means, either by plane, or with a ferry from Denmark. I'll give you an overview for each.

By Ferry

Currently, there is only one ferry operator *"Smyril Line"* (www.smyrilline.com), which can bring you, and, if you need, your car/camper/caravan/motorbike or bicycle over the North Atlantic Ocean to Iceland and back. A very big and comfortable cruise-ferry called "*MS Norröna II*" is sailing from *Hirtshals* (Denmark) [🌎 57.596246, 9.974747] through *Tórshavn* (Faroe Islands) [🌎 62.007758, -6.765710] to *Seydisfjordur* (Iceland) [🌎 65.263343, -14.002618] weekly. They sail all year round and have: "Winter Season" (Nov-Mar), "Low Season" (1x weekly, Apr + Oct), "Mid-Season (1x weekly, May + Sep) and "High Season" (2x weekly, Jun-Aug). In the "High Season" "*MS Norröna II*" makes 2x sails, first on Saturdays, it goes to *Tórshavn* (Faroe Islands) and back, then on Tuesdays, it sails again to *Tórshavn*, and then farther to *Seydisfjordur* (Iceland). To remember it easier, the ferry sails 1x once per week to Iceland around year, but in "High Season" it makes an extra trip to Faroe Islands. "*Smyril Line*" is the Faroe Islands' company, was founded in 1982, has a relatively new (operates since 2003) and large 8 deck ferry "*MS Norröna II*" worth of ~€93,4 million for 1482 passengers (318 cabins, 1012 beds) and 800 cars (or 130 trailers), and for cargo capacity 3,250 tones, with lane 1830 m and length 165.7 m, and cruise speed 21 knots (38.9 km/h) operated by 14 main crew staff (3 on the bridge, 5 in the engine-room and 6 at the deck) with up to 118 total number of people in the crew. The ferry has everything to make your journey pleasant: (deck 2) swimming pool, sauna and fitness room; (deck 5) reception/info desk, cinema, playground, Naust, the Dinner and tax-free shop; (deck 6) Norröna buffet and Simmer Dim; (deck 7) hot tubes, teen room, conference room; (deck 8) Sky Bar and FIFA pitch.

There are a few different types of cabins in the ferry, I will review them in detail:

1st Class

Deluxe cabins – the most comfortable and expensive cabins in the ferry, with one double bed and one sofa bed, can accommodate 2-4 people. Each cabin has 2 windows, big TV, minibar (included in the price), toilet/bathroom, fruit basket, 240 V electricity.

Family cabins – are cabins for big families, can accommodate up to 6 people, and consist of two interconnected rooms, one has a double bed, another 4 additional beds, two of them can be transformed into sofas. There is a big TV, toilet/bathroom, minibar (not included in the price), 240 V electricity.

The suites – are huge cabins, resembling more an apartment than a ship cabin, they have a big living room with TV and a large sofa with armchairs, a bigger bathroom with a bathtub, and a separate bedroom with a king-size double bed, additional TV and window. Minibar is included in the price.

2nd Class

4 berth cabins with/without window – cabins of the middle class, designed for 4 people travelling together, have 4 berths, two of them can be transformed into sofas, WC, shower, hairdryer, TV, minibar (not included in the price), 240 V electricity.

Double bed cabins – comfortable cabins (deck 7) with a window, WC, shower, hairdryer, TV, 240 V electricity, can be booked for two or one person.

2 berth cabins with/without a window - spacious cabins with two lower beds, which can be transformed into sofas, with WC, shower, hairdryer, TV, 240 V electricity, for one or two persons.

Cabins for disabled – well equipped cabins for wheelchair (deck 5 and 6), they have specially made sink, mirror and a toilet designed for handicapped passengers, and the door that leads into the cabin is wide enough for a wheelchair to roll in. The cabin has the same equipment as the other cabins such as bed linen, towels, hairdryer, 240 V electricity, TV. These cabins are only available with window and can be booked for 2-4 people.

3rd Class

Couchettes – cheapest cabins shared for 6 people (deck 2, below car deck), there are 6 bunk beds in each couchette compartment. With your couchette, it is always included a breakfast in "The Diner" restaurant, unless you booked the whole couchette compartment (6 people) as a family or a group, then it is not included, however, if you want, you can book your meal separately. Bed linen is not included in the couchette price, but you can book it separately for €9 per person, but a lot of people sleep there in their own sleeping bags, as I did, it is totally fine. WC, showers are in the corridor, near your cabin. There is luggage storage on deck 2 or 7. The boxes are in two sizes: the large box is 88cm (D), 60cm (H) and 40cm (W) and the smaller one is 78cm (D), 40cm (H) and 30cm (W). The cost for using the boxes is DKK 10 for the small one and DKK 20 for the bigger one. It costs every time the box is opened. Please, note that single couchette compartments cannot be locked, this is why there are storage rooms, however, your section with a few compartments is locked with your magnetic card.

I will give you a few examples for *Norröna*'s fare prices, that you have an idea how much the journey may cost you. Please, note that if you go to Iceland, and will agree to stay at least 3 days in Faroe Islands, on your way back, for example, "*Smyril Line*" normally gives a discount. You can see all the prices during booking process or in their booklet online (you can download it as pdf) (www.issuu.com/smyrilline.com/docs/smyril line catalog 2019).

Hirtshals (Denmark) - *Seydisfjordur* (Iceland), one-way, through *Tórshavn* (Faroe Islands):

x1 person in a couchette compartment – €295 (High Season), €200 (Low Season);

x1 person + a car in a couchette compartment – €655 (High Season), €350 (Low Season);

x2 persons + a car in a couchette compartment – €875 (High Season), €505 (Low Season);

x1 person in a 2 berths cabin – €635 (High Season), €315 (Low Season);
x1 person + a car in a 2 berths cabin – €995 (High Season), €465 (Low Season);
x2 persons + a car in a 2 berths cabin – €1215 (High Season), €620 (Low Season);

In *Hirtshals* (Denmark), people usually arrive a day before the ferry's departure, be that the case with you, there is a nice big and modern camping site and cottages at the city's border, near the seashore and close to the harbor (www.hirtshals-camping.dk/en) (€18, WC, shower (DKK5), free Wi-Fi, small shop, children playground, kitchen, dining room, fresh bread in mornings) [🌍 57.586384, 9.945515]. If you will decide to spend a few days in Faroe Islands, there is a nice modern and clean campsite at the *Tórshavn*'s shore, ~10 m from the ocean [🌍 62.016905, -6.755153], just ~20 min walk from the harbor, where *Norröna* comes (see www.visittorshavn.fo, then "where to stay" > "camping", DKK95, WC, showers (DKK10 for 4 min), kitchen, dining room, free Wi-Fi). In *Seydisfjordur* (Iceland), there is also a big camping site, close to the harbor, city center and shops (www.visitseydisfjordur.com/project/camping-and-caravan-site) [🌍 65.260432, -14.011248] (ISK1,600, + ISK333 tax, WC, kitchen, dining room, showers (ISK100 for 2 min), free Wi-Fi).

By Plane

There are many airlines (~30, -1 for "**WOW**", it was a nice low-cost Icelandic carrier, it ceased its operations on March 28th, 2019), which fly directly from the Europe's mainland, UK or North America to Iceland, but most of them provide service only in high and shoulder seasons, and just a few fly all year around. You can select what fits you the best in terms of price, time and comfort by using your favorite flight search and book online service or App, e.g. "**Skyscanner**" (www.skyscanner.net), or "**Google Flights**" (www.google.com/flights), or "**Kayak**" (www.kayak.com), or "**Swoodoo**" (www.swoodoo.com). There is only one international airport in Iceland, which is called "*Keflavík Airport*" (KEF) (www.isavia.is/en/keflavik-airport) [🌍 63.996977, -22.623809], located ~50 km from Reykjavik (**road 41**). There are a few different buses operate between the airport and *Reykjavik*. There is a "**FlyBus**" shuttle going hourly around a clock (www.re.is/flybus), you have to book your ticket and seat online (ISK3,499 one-way ticket, ~45 min journey, a big white in color comfortable bus with Wi-Fi), and the bus can bring you directly to your hotel, hostel or city center. The second option would be to use a normal city bus by "**Straeto**" (www.straeto.is/en), **line 55**, *KEF Airport - Reykjanesbær -Keilir - Fjörður – Reykjavík* (ticket one-way: ~ISK1,840, they go every 1-2 hours and only from 6:35 till 22:55 Mo-Fri, and Sat-Sun, the bus operates only between *KEF Airport – Fjörður* [🌐 64.067703, -21.957494], at very South of *Reykjavik*), there are 2x bus stops ("S" system, "Straeto") near the airport, one for departures (~100 m left from the main exit from the building) [🌐 63.99704, -22.62488], the second nearby for arrivals [🌐 63.99695, -22.62791]. The third option is to use another transfer shuttle bus "**Airport Direct**" (www.airportdirect.is), one-way ISK3,590 + ISK1,200, if you want to be transferred directly to your hotel. The fourth option is to use a taxi, which, considering the distance (~50 km to the city center), it might cost you a lot of money (~ISK15,000-17,000), depending on the company, season, how many seats in the car.

WHERE TO STAY

There are many different types of accommodation in Iceland, but they are quite expensive, although, everything isn't cheap in Iceland, therefore, I will review in this book only camping sites/huts, to my opinion, this is the best way to explore beautiful nature of Iceland, to sleep outdoor, under polar sky in your tent, and to meet wonderful people from all around the world. All camping sites and mountain huts will be reviewed in detail with prices and facilities at each sightseeing, trek point, if there are any campsites available nearby.

In the Icelandic capital, *Reykjavik*, there is a central super-big, most expensive and modern 5-stars camping site "*Reykjavik Campsite*", located just in the city center, close to the shopping and dining streets (~20-30 min walk), and the harbor, in a green district, in front of the city's swimming pool [🌐 64.145838, -21.875752] (www.reykjavikcampsite.is) (ISK2,400, WC, showers, kitchen, big dining room, free Wi-Fi, long term luggage storage (ISK600-3,500), Long term storage flattened bike boxes (ISK3,500), washing/drying (each ISK700), bike rental (ISK2,000), free bookings and pick up for excursions and a bus to the *Keflavik* airport, information board).

Figure 1 Panoramic views at Frostastaðavatn Lake (image #1), Bláhnúkur Mount trail (image #2), colorful rainbow-like Mount Brennisteinsalda and Bláhnúkur Mount in the center (image #3)

Figure 2 Panoramic views to the valleys and lava fields from Bláhnúkur Mount trail

HOW TO COMMUTE

The best most comfortable way to commute through Iceland is either by bus (read below) or with your own or rented car (especially during Winter, Early Spring and Late Autumn seasons), even better when your car is a 4WD Jeep, then you can reach places, where otherwise you won't make it. Of course, with a conventional 2WD car you will see majority of sightseeing on Iceland ("Ring" road N1), no doubt, however, if you want to see its heart and soul, you have to go to Highlands, where's no civilization, only rough gravel and stony off-roads with a lot of river crossing without any bridges, by fording, or propelling through nasty black volcanic sand and lava fields like gigantic 3D mazes.

There are ~6 major bus companies operating through the whole Iceland. There is a very nice official public transport website www.publictransport.is.

"*STRAETO*" (www.straeto.is) is a main and cheapest public buses operator on Iceland, which covers the capital area and majority of destinations on Iceland, has night buses in *Reykjavik* and around, and buses connecting the airport *Keflavik* with the capital. Buses are yellow in color and have numbers, and bus stops have big yellow letter "S" in a red circle. There is an App "*Straeto*", which you can download from **App Store** or **Google Play**, and buy tickets, plan your trip and see the bus schedule, you can even watch buses location in real time via their GPS. Prices are the following: in the Capital Area, single ticket ISK460 (night fare, ISK 920), 1 day pass ISK1,700, 3 days pass ISK4,000, 1 month card ISK12,300, a ticket to the *Keflavik* airport ISK1,840, *Reykjavik-Borgarnes* ISK1,840, *Reykjavik-Akureyri* ISK10,120, *Reykjavik-Vik* ISK6,440, *Reykjavik-Skaftafell* ISK10,120, *Reykjavik-Höfn* ISK13,340, *Akureyri-Egilsstadir* ISK8,280, *Akureyri-Husavik* ISK2,760.

"*STERNA*" (www.icelandbybus.is) is a small bus company commuting in the South coast of Iceland, between *Reykjavik – Vik – Glacier Lagoon*, and in **Highlands**, between *Reykjavik - Landmannalaugar*, and *Reykjavik – Þórsmörk*, *Reykjavik – Skógar*. There is one morning's bus daily in each direction and one in the afternoons back to *Reykjavik*. You can buy a single ticket via a booking system at their website, or you can buy a bus passport, which allows you to hop on and off any time on the bus while you are hiking, at bus stops in towns, villages and camping sites. For **Highland Pass** (*Reykjavik - Landmannalaugar, Reykjavik – Þórsmörk, Reykjavik – Skógar* and return), it is valid from June 10th - September 15th, a bus passport costs ISK13,900 and for the **South Coast Pass** (*Reykjavík - Glacier Lagoon* and return), ISK19,900, it is valid for up to 60 days, from July 1st - August 31st. They also offer the **Fimmvörðuháls Mountain Pass** (*Reykjavik – Þórsmörk, Reykjavik – Skógar*), ISK12,900, and the **Ultimate Bus Passport** (it includes all routes), ISK27,900. To guarantee a seat on the bus, you need to check in at least 24 hours prior to departure at the website.

"*TREX*" (www.trex.is) is in short, a bus company for hikers, it runs 4WD buses, which capable to go to Highlands, face volcanic black sand tracks and ford quite deep rivers. It offers daily 2x buses to 2x "Hiking Meccas", either in *Þórsmörk* (14.06 – 8.09.2019, *Reykjavík* (City Hall: **7:30**, **12:30**, Camping: **7:45**, **12:45**) – *Þórsmörk* (Básar: **11:45**, **16:45** and Langidalur: **12:00**, **17:00**), rates: *Reykjavík* > *Þórsmörk*, one-way ticket ISK9,000, with return ISK15,200, Hikers bus pass ISK15,300, or in *Landmannalaugar* (21.06 – 8.09.2019), *Reykjavík* (City Hall: **7:30**, **12:30**, Camping: **7:45**, **12:45**) – *Landmannalaugar* (Camping: **11:45**, **16:45**), rates: *Reykjavík* > *Landmannalaugar*, one-way ticket ISK9,400, with return ISK17,300, Hikers bus pass ISK15,300). And return buses are from *Þórsmörk* at **12:30** and **18:00**, that you are in *Reykjavik* at around **18:30** and **22:00**; and *Landmannalaugar* at **14:30** and **18:00**, and you are back in *Reykjavik* at **18:30** and **22:00**, correspondently. The company also offers "**hikers bus passes**", which give you some flexibility, e.g. you hike from a place "A" to a place "B", the hikers bus pass will allow you to have a bus to the place "A", then hike as long as you need, and then to be picked up at the place "B" at any time you want it (during online booking you have to specify all dates and time, but it is easy to change them, if you need it, via email info@trex.is or just talk to a bus driver on the next available bus). For example, if you want to do the "*Laugavegur*" hike (*Landmannalaugar* – *Þórsmörk*, ~54 km, 3-4 days hike), then you book a bus seat for *Reykjavik* – *Landmannalaugar* (ISK7,650), you may stay in *Landmannalaugar* for 3-4 days to explore this beautiful area with colorful mountains, and then hike to *Þórsmörk* within 4 days, and have your bus back to the capital from *Þórsmörk* (ISK7,650). Such arrangements "TREX" offers for the *Fimmvörðuháls* hike (*Þórsmörk* – *Skógar*, ~23 km, 9 hr hiking, you can do it in one day or in two), and for the whole trek *Laugavegur* + *Fimmvörðuháls* (*Landmannalaugar* – *Skógar*, 77 km, 4-6 days hike); of course, you can decide yourself, which direction you hike: *Landmannalaugar* – *Skógar*, or in the reverse direction.

There is another bus company "*Thule Travel*" (www.thuletravel.is), which can bring you to Highlands, they offer a pass *Reykjavík* – *Landmannalaugar*, and *Reykjavík* – *Þórsmörk* with return, it operates from June 15th to September 15th, ISK15,800, with one bus daily; plus, it offers a Golden Hikers Pass (*Reykjavik* – *Landmannalaugar*, *Reykjavík* – *Þórsmörk*, and *Reykjavík* – *Skógar*) for only ISK14,000, it is valid from June 15th to September 15th.

There is one more bus company, which works for Highland hikers, "*Reykjavik Excursions*" – "*Iceland on your Own*" (www.re.is/iceland-on-your-own), they offer a **Hiking Pass** with the same routes (*Reykjavik* – *Landmannalaugar*, [14 June –

15 September], *Reykjavík – Þórsmörk*, [1 June – 20 September], and *Reykjavík – Skógar* [1 July – 31 August]) for ISK14,000.

And the last bus company I want to review here is *"SBA"* (www.sba.is), which has a very interesting scheduled bus route (not a tour): *Reykjavík* (BSÍ Bus Terminal, Mon, Wed, Fr, Sun, 8:00) – *Kjölur* – *Akureyri* (18:30) going through **Highlands** by many interesting sights like: *Geysir, Gullfoss, Hvítárnes, Hveravellir,* and using a dirt bumpy Highland **road 35** (**F35**), which is by itself an adventure; one-way ticket for the whole route is ISK17,900.

HOW TO SURVIVE AS AN ADVENTUROUS HIKER

You can't visit Iceland without hiking there at all, at least a few kilometers; even at most touristic sightseeing with good facilities, paved roads and ice-cream, there will be plenty of short hikes around to see the natural beauty in full scale and from different perspective. However, Iceland has become in recent years popular for real challenging hiking and multiday trekking through inhabitable, wild and rough landscapes. There are many examples on **YouTube** now, when brave people cross the whole island from South's shore to Northern fjords (~600 km) on foot, going through **Highlands**, and completing the journey within 3 weeks' time. If you decide to venture yourself to such adventurous, if not to say, dangerous, multiday trekking, I would suggest a **few paramount things**:

1) please, make sure you carry enough water and food, and remember that water is your priority: without water your body can properly function only ~3 days, without food – 3 weeks, in general, small rivers and streams have drinkable clean and tasty water (if they are not polluted by close farms or construction work), however, big and fast glacial rivers, especially in Highlands, have undrinkable water, it is milky-bluish in color, and has a lot of chemicals and sediments, not good for your stomach;

2) you better have a proper GPS navigator and updated off-line maps (in many places in Iceland, especially in Highlands, there is no mobile signal or it is too weak, however, satellite GPS signal you can get **almost** everywhere and at any weather conditions), and either a power bank and/or a solar charger, that your navigator will not run away from battery; to correctly locate yourself in lava fields, endless hills, volcanic deserts, high mountains is essential for survival, especially in Highlands, where in tall lava fields (5-7 m high), you won't see properly landmarks and the trail;

3) if you know, there will be sparse water, or if you aren't sure whether it will be any water at all on your way, please, try to save water while you hike, to do so, do not cook (!!!), or cook less, e.g. every second day only, or cook if you found a good water stream (but still have at least 2x gas cartridges by 100 g, a light mini-

stove and a light titanium cooking set), cooking requires at least 1 L (½ L for e.g. cooking pasta + ½ L for cleaning cooking gears) of precious water daily, instead, bring with you: fat cheese, smoke-dried sausages and meat, Icelandic dried fish ("*hardfiskur*"), different sets of nuts, dried fruits, chocolates, cookies, dried bread, protein bars, honey ...etc;

4) remember, if your body weight is ~70-80 kg, and you carry a heavy backpack (~20-30 kg) hiking through a difficult terrain for 8 hours, you will burn daily at least 3000 kcal (not 2000 kcal as for normal conditions), but most probably, it will be close to 4000 kcal or even more (~400-500 kcal/hour); you also have to bear in mind that your body contains some kgs of fat tissue, which can be gradually used during intensive hiking, the energy is released from fat is about 7 kcal/g or 7000 kcal/kg; if you do a serious hike and burn 4000 kcal daily, technically, it will be very difficult to restore spent energy with only food in your backpack (a package of professional daily meal for hikers usually contains ~400-800 kcal, if you eat it twice daily, plus protein bars, fruits, nuts, you won't be able to reach 4000 kcal every day, though, unavoidably you will burn your own fat, losing a few kgs at the end of a 1-2 weeks hike; to conclude, if you have some extra weight as body fat, at the end of the day, it is not so bad for enduring hiking, especially in Iceland, it will literally sustain you on long trails, plus, will better insulate you in the "ice and fire" land;

5) the same with water, your daily water consumption will be at least 3 L (not 2 L as for normal conditions), but for the worst scenario, your "survival" minimum water consumption should be around 1 L daily;

6) please, bring with you a good water filter (!!!), - at the worst scenario, after filtration, setting sediment down (2-4 hr) and boiling (5-10 min) you can drink milky glacial water from Highlands' rivers – it should be fine for a day or two;

7) it also could be very useful to know how to collect precipitated water from morning's fogs and rains, by using your tent, cooking gears, waterproof bags, your raincoat or jacket;

8) please, be aware that hiking in Highlands requires properly selected clothes as it is colder there than in Southern or Northern regions of Iceland, the night temperature can easily drop close to zero levels, even in the middle of Summer, it is also very windy there, serious sand or rain storms can be formed in Highlands within hours, if not minutes in time-scale. Make sure you have enough dry wool or synthetic clothes, which can well insulate you from cold and rain, and if wet, dry fast. For most conditions a 3-layer outfit is enough for hiking in Iceland, however, when it is too windy and cold, a fourth layer should be added. Please, be aware, unfortunately, almost every year a few hikers die in Highlands mostly due to hypothermia;

9) if you know the way **in** and **out** of your hiking route, you know where to go, - **you are safe** (!!!), so, please, before challenging yourself to any long hiking adventures, get to know your main trail, your alternative trails, if any, landmarks,

mountain huts, campings, where you can get water and have shelters... etc, do some at least minimalistic research of your itinerary before you go hiking, read guidebooks, watch **YouTube**, play with **Google Maps** and **Street View**, study the GPS-located trails via a nice "**WikiLoc**" website (www.wikiloc.com);

10) If you have a choice to hike alone or in a group, do it in the group; if you have a choice to hike with a guide or without, do it with the guide; if you got lost due to fog, low clouds, heavy rain, stop where you are, put your tent and wait for weather to be cleaned, then continue;

11) if you go solo for a serious day or multiday hike, please, inform rangers, camping personnel, or a **search and rescue** team, about your plans; there is a nice online service www.safetravel.is, where you can post your hiking itinerary and time schedule, and if you do not report yourself that you've completed the route safely, the search and rescue team will organize a search mission.

12) **a good practice** is when you go for a just-a-few-hours hike into an unknown place, to carry with you extra warm and rainproof clothes, a first aid kit, enough water and food provision as like you go for a long-day hike; and when you go for a day hike, to bring with you stuff as like you go for two days hike.

Figure 3 Panoramic views of rainbow-like colorful volcano Brennisteinsalda (image #1) and a reddish crater Stútur and Norðurnámur Mount behind (image #2)

Figure 4 Hidden secret lake near a rainbow-like colorful volcano Brennisteinsalda (image #1) and two hikers are traversing a massive lava field (image #2) at the foot of this mount

LANDMANNALAUGAR
KEY SIGHTSEEING

Landmannalaugar – is [*ISL*, "*People's Pools/Baths*"] an Icelandic hiking "Mecca", a must-go for any nature lovers, adventure seekers, photographers; the reason – stunning unearthly beautiful rhyolite and basalt colorful mountains and volcanoes, since the region is highly volcanically active, it forms here a full spectrum of dazzling colors, from red, pink, yellow and green, to violet, blue and turquoise. It is here, the most popular in Iceland 4-days hiking trail *Laugavegur* is ending, connecting *Landmannalaugar* and *Þórsmörk*, [*ISL*, "*Valley of Thor*"], and a huge *Skógafoss* waterfall at the oceanic shore, just over the mountains and glaciers, through the *Fimmvörðuháls* trail between the two glaciers *Eyjafjallajökull* and *Mýrdalsjökull*. It is a key part of *Fjallabak* **Nature Reserve** [*ISL*, "*Mountain's Back*"], which was founded in 1979 and has 470 km² territory (~20x25 km). There are many lava fields, the closest to the camping site is *Laugahraun*, which was formed by volcanic eruption in 1477 by *Torfajökull* volcano (stratovolcano, huge caldera 18x12 km, fissure swarm 30x40 km, it forms the largest geothermal area in Iceland of about 150 km²), as well as other lava fields nearby, like *Námshraun*, and *Norðurnámshraun*, however, its largest eruption was in ~870. The area, its mountain floor, was formed about 10 million years ago.

There is a nice and big camping site (at ~590 m a.s.l.), just in the heart of *Landmannalaugar* [🌍 63.990627, -19.060306] with WC, hot showers (extra costs ~ISK500 for those who do not stay overnight in the camp, but free who paid a night, ~ISK2,000), dining and cooking place (a huge tent with tables and benches), a small basic food and travel gears shop and cafeteria in 2 school buses. There are 2 areas for tents; one is very stony, another, usually, is very wet as its location is close to streams and swampy grassland. Just over the corner of main facility and ticket buildings, there is a wonderful natural hot spring, where you can bath for free after a long hike. There are 3 parking lots; 2 are very close to the campground, and the third one is ~800 m outside the camp, for vehicles which can't ford 2 rivers (one is quite deep). To get to the heart and soul of the Highlands – *Landmannalaugar*, you need to drive a 4WD car, fully insured for roughest off-roads of Highlands. There are 3 major routes to the place: 1) from North, near the waterfall *Goðafoss*, from the road 1, take a dirt **road 842** going South, then stony and rocky Highland roads **F26**, **F208**, **F224** (~266 km from the ring road and *Goðafoss*); 2) from West, e.g. from *Reykjavik* – take roads 1, **26**, *Landmannaleið*, **F208**, **F224** (~180 km from *Reykjavik*, ~95 km from the ring road); 3) from South, near *Kirkjubæjarklaustur*, roads **209/208**, **210**, **F210**, **F233**, **F208**, **F224** (~75 km from the ring road). For those who have no 4WD cars, there are several buses going there daily from the capital by different operators, with possibility to return at the same day, if you need it, please, see updated schedules and do booking in advance at the web site below (e.g. ticket range: one way ~ISK 8,000-9,400, with return ~ISK 15,000-17,300, you can also have a pass with discounts, e.g. "Highland Hikers Passport" ~ISK 14,000): "**Reykjavik Excursions**" (www.re.is/iceland-on-your-own), "**Iceland by Bus**", previously it was named "**Sterna**" (www.icelandbybus.is), "**TREX**" (www.trex.is/tour/landmannalaugar), "**Thule Travel** (www.thuletravel.is/landmannalaugar).

Frostastaðavatn – [*ISL, "frosted lake"*] is a great truly Highlands' lake (~2x3 km) with turquoise waters, surrounded by volcanoes, craters and lava fields, and located in the heart of *Landmannalaugar* [64.019902, -19.059987], ~1 hr hike (~3 km) from the camping site [63.990627, -19.060306] with WC, hot showers (extra costs ~ISK500 for those who do not stay overnight in the camp, but free who paid a night, ~ISK2,000), dining and cooking place (a huge tent with tables and benches), a small basic food and travel gears shop and cafeteria in 2 school buses. It is also very close to the famous *Laugavegur* hiking trek. For those, who are staying a few days at the campsite, there are dozens of hiking trails at the lake's Eastern bank: hikes around *Námshraun* and *Norðurnámshraun* lava fields, near the picturesque volcanic crater *Stútur* (623 m), which you can climb up, there is a nice viewpoint nearby [64.013864, -19.046049], hikes to a mount *Norðurnámur* (792 m), and a hike (~3 km from the lake's viewpoint and road **F208**) to a smaller lake *Ljótipollur*, located Northeast from the lake. Basically, anywhere you go, you see trodden trails either nicely marked or unmarked, but clearly visible; one can hike here for weeks, and it won't be enough.

Stútur – is a quite big (~60 m diameter) and picturesque volcanic crater (623 m a.s.l.), located in **Highlands**, in *Landmannalaugar* region, near road **F208** [64.013118, -19.040811], leading to the camping site [63.990861, -19.060193], ~3.3 km (turn to **F224**). You can hike it on the top and walk around its rim; there are marked trails for ascending and descending the crater and nearby many other trails. The hike is easy, moderately steep, but in wet conditions it might be muddy and slippery. The crater is surrounded by lava fields covered by ancient 1000-years old moss (do not walk on it!!!). There is a parking lot 300 m from the crater with a nice viewpoint [64.013774, -19.045686] back to the crater and beneath to a lake *Frostastaðavatn*.

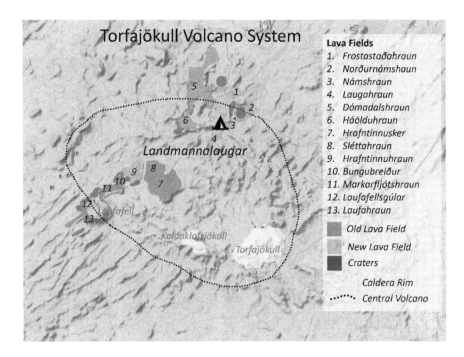

Figure 5 *Landmannalaugar is a huge volcanic caldera (yellow dotted line) of the Torfajökull volcanic system (last eruption in 1477 CE), representing a central volcano area (black dotted line) with many ~13 lava fields (green regions) and numerous craters (red areas). I made this map based on information provided by a nice Catalogue of Icelandic Volcanoes (www.icelandicvolcanoes.is), the topo map of the area is taken from OpenStreet Maps Database (www.openstreetmap.org), the cycling map layer.*

Hekla – is another big iconic volcano in Iceland. It is a rather tall (1491 m high a.s.l.) stratovolcano (classical cone-like shape) situated in South of Iceland [🌍 63.99189, -19.66722], just 90 min drive from *Reykjavik*. It is very active, last eruption was February-March 2000. Over the last 1000 years *Hekla* erupted about 20-30 times, forming 10% (5 km³) of all volcanic tephra and lava (8 km³) on Iceland. In the Middle Age, Europeans believed that *Hekla* is a gateway to hell. During the "sleeping" periods, *Hekla* is usually covered with snow and glaciers (see the picture above, volcano at the left side). It is quite often one can experience here around *Hekla* small earthquakes with magnitude of 2, when it is erupting, it shakes with magnitude 3. The longest (1 year) recorded eruption was in 1947, starting at 29 of March and ending by April 1948. People believe that longer *Hekla* is sleeping, more catastrophic will be its next eruption. In prehistoric time, *Hekla* was one of the most active volcanoes, it erupted in 950 BC (*Hekla* 3, **H3**), in 2310-20 BC (**H4**), in 3900 BC and in 5050 BC (**H5**). **H3** eruption was enormous, throwing 7.3 km³ of volcanic elements into the air, and cooling down Europe for a few years after. *Hekla* eruptions 3, 4 and 5 formed largest layers 80% of all ash and tephra on Iceland since Ice Age. Over the last 7000 years 1/3 of all volcanic ash covered Scandinavia, Ireland, UK and Germany was coming from *Hekla*. It erupted 4 times in 20th century, and people believe that in 21th century its activity is increasing, and eruptions may occur every 10 years. Nevertheless, *Hekla* is very popular for hiking; trails lead to the summit; the walk up takes 3-4 hours. The volcano can be reached by buses going to *Landmannalaugar* [🌍 63.993944, -19.058661] colorful mountains, just 30 km East from the volcano. *Hekla* for hiking can be approached from North; there are 2 hiking trails, which start from *Landmannaleid* road (**F225**) at 2 different places [🌍 64.07371, -19.52914] and [🌍 64.08509, -19.61693]; while **F225** is connected with the road **26** *Landvegur*, and then with the ring road at South. The hiking trail (~13 km one way from the road **F225** to the summit) to *Hekla* is going through a volcanic crater named *Raudaskal* (597 m a.s.l.) [🌍 64.03768, -19.56781]. The road *Landmannaleid* from West to East leads to *Fridland* and *Fjallabaki Park*, towards to *Landmannalaugar* colorful mountains [🌍 63.993944, -19.058661]. West from *Hekla*, about 20 km, on the **road 26**, there are a camping site (WC, hot showers, children playground) [🌍 63.993284, -20.012716], and a hotel *Leirubakki* (www.leirubakki.is) [🌍 63.992691, -20.013219] with a shop and a petrol station N1, and a *Hekla* museum and info center, in addition, a natural hot bath nearby, called *Viking Pool* [🌍 63.990502, -20.013542]. To get here is very easy, since buses, connecting *Reykjavik* and

Landmannalaugar colorful mountains, stop by the place daily, e.g. tour buses from "**TREX**" (www.trex.is/tour/landmannalaugar), and "**Iceland by bus**" (www.icelandbybus.is).

Skógafoss – is a very beautiful, powerful and tall (60 m high) waterfall located in high cliffs of Iceland's South coastline and the ring road [🌐 63.531795, -19.511501], taking its waters from *Skógar* river, which delivers melted icy water from two glaciers, *Eyjafjallajökull* at the left side, a rather small glacier (peak, volcano, 1651 m a.s.l.) but with a very famous volcano *Eyjafjallajökull* [🌐 63.633000, -19.600000], which erupted in 2010 (Apr 15 – May 20), causing enormous disruption of flights across Europe and Atlantic ocean for a week, and *Mýrdalsjökull* glacier at the right side, many-folds bigger in size than the previous one (1495 m a.s.l with a subglacial famous volcano *Katla*, [🌐 63.646517, -19.130376], 1512 m a.s.l., las eruption Oct-Nov 1918). You can come very close to the waterfall being literally enveloped with clouds of water spray, heavy sounds and rainbows at sunny days. There is a viewing platform on the waterfall's top, you have to climb by a metal staircase up with 527 steps, ~60 m high, which is quite a fitness. There is a simple campsite (WC, hot showers ~ISK300, no kitchen, no shelters, ~ISK1,500 per person, could be overcrowded as the place is very touristic) just in front of the fall, you can sleep in your tent under its melody, a few parking lots, hostels, hotels, restaurants, bars, cafes, shops. There is a small food shop and touristic gears shop in the building of a big canteen/restaurant called "**Fossbúð**" (www.hotelskogar.is/fossbud-restaurant, lamb soup, ~1,000 *ISK*, fish & chips, ~1,500 *ISK*, salads, pasta, nudes, beer, ~1,000 *ISK*, wine, dessert … etc) [🌐 63.526916, -19.509257], not far from waterfall and the campsite. In the canteen you can have a breakfast, lunch or dinner (less expensive than in other 1st row-to-waterfall restaurants), but also you can buy some fresh "to-go" snacks for your hikes (I give this info because in many travel guides, they say there is no any grocery shops around, where you can buy food supply for your hikes, though, it is not really true). You may also find closer to the ring road a few mobile fast-food shops in vans with even cheaper food. And lastly, there is a big modern cafeteria and snack shop (www.skogasafn.is/skogar-museum/skogakaffi-cafe), not so far from the waterfall (~1.5 km) [🌐 63.526007, -19.492744] in the **Skogar Technical museum** of old cars and ship, plus, there is a shop for travel gears, souvenirs and traditional Icelandic and hiking clothes. There is also one of the most popular and challenging hiking trails in Iceland called *Fimmvörðuháls* (read "Multiday Trekking" chapter), it is ~25 km long and can be walked by a day or two, and it ends up in a region called *Thorsmork*, a place with name *Básar*. There are a lot of public buses going here:

Reykjavík – Höfn, **line 51** (www.straeto.is), or with hiking bus passes with return, e.g. *"Fimmvorduhals* **Hikers Passport**" ~ISK12,900, or **"South Coast Passport"**, *Reykjavík – Glacier Lagoon*, ISK19,990, or a ticket with return *Reykjavík – Skógar*, ISK10,400 (www.icelandbybus.is) or **line 21**, ~ISK15,000 with return (www.re.is/iceland-on-your-own).

Seljalandsfoss – is another "must see" waterfall (www.seljalandsfoss.is), which is located [🌐 63.615507, -19.988510] just 30 km West from *Skogafoss* by the ring road in South Iceland. It is similar high as *Skogafoss*, about 63-65 m, and takes its waters from the *Seljalands* river, powered by melted ice of the *Eyjafjallajokull* glacier above. The waterfall is well known for its interesting and unique feature as visitors can walk behind the waterfall and go around it by a small cave. Considering the size of the waterfall, and amount of water falling from above, it is breathtaking experience. The only advise would be is to wear a water-proof jacket or a raincoat, and good hiking boots, as rocks nearby the waterfall are wet, and well mossed and thus very slippery. Very close, ~1 km from *Seljalandsfoss*, there is another (40 m high) waterfall called *Gljúfrafoss* [*ISL,* "*one who lives in a canyon*"] [🌐 63.620849, -19.986246], well hidden in a canyon, rocks and caves, but worth to visit and explore, plus, a smaller unnamed one nearby. In front of two waterfalls, there is a nice camping site *Hamragarðar* (ISK1,500) with Wi-Fi, kitchen, dining and resting room, WC, hot showers (extra ISK300 for 3 min), but could be overcrowded, with many cars and campers, thus muddy. There are also a few short hiking trails going uphill, to the top of waterfalls and around; definitely, they are worth to explore and stay at the place a day or two. You can get here by many buses operating at South, e.g. **line 51** (www.straeto.is), check at (www.publictransport.is).

Reynisdrangar – are lonely standing beautifully shaped basalt rock formations [🌐 63.399339, -19.031471] at the ocean shore near a small but modern town called *Vik* [🌐 63.419478, -19.006494] at the Southern coast of Iceland. These giant rock pillars can be easily sighted from *Reynisfjara* – a popular black sand beach located 5-min walk from the town center. An alternative way to see these stacks from above is by climbing a big (200 m a.s.l.) mountain *Reynisfjall* nearby, there are circular trails at its top (~3 km one way, an easy walk), starting at the parking lot here [🌐 63.418553, -19.014089]. There are Icelandic folk tales, which tell stories about these massive rocks: one says there were two trolls stoned by rising sun when they tried to capture a ship; another says these two trolls murdered a woman, and her husband hunted and tricked them down, to stay off-shade that they converted into stones. In the town *Vik* you can find everything: gasoline station N1, big food mall and "**IceWear**" center (www.icewear.is) with traditional Icelandic wool clothes, hiking gears, sportive shoes, travel accessories, *Víkurskáli* – a nice big restaurant/canteen with self-service, "*Strondin*" Bistro & Bar (www.strondin.is), a stylish newly built (opened in 2018) brewpub *Smiðjan Brugghús* (www.smidjanbrugghus.is/en/home), where you can get 180 g grilled burgers and has 10 Icelandic craft beers on draft, "*Soup Company*" restaurant (www.thesoupcompanyiceland.com), where you can taste a "*red hot lava*" soup, and in the same building there is "*Icelandic Lava Show*" (www.icelandiclavashow.com), where you can see, smell and hear how real hot molted lava flows in close proximity to you, nearby *Vínbúðin* (shop for alcoholic

beverages), swimming pool, ATM and bank, and a huge camping ground [63.419390, -18.995358] (~ISK 1,750, hot shower ~ISK 200, free Wi-Fi, kitchen and dining room, laundry service, www.vikcamping.is) at the foot of a rock cliff with a famous *Víkurkirkja* Lutheran church. For many tourists, riding an Icelandic strong horse along a volcanic black sand beach in front of gigantic rock pillars at distance is a long-desired dream, well, not in *Vik*, you can make it true here. To get to *Vik*, if you travel on foot, is very easy, since majority public and tour buses commuting at South, stop here, e.g. **line 51** (www.straeto.is), or with (www.icelandbybus.is), check timetables and routes at (www.publictransport.is).

Figure 6 *Panoramic views of smoky and smelly hot springs near a rainbow-like colorful volcano Brennisteinsalda (image #1,3), an awkward rock formation resembling an erected phallus (image #2) and mossed lava field in front of colorful mount ridge (image #4)*

Figure 7 Major 1/2 day and full day hikes in Landmannalaugar colorful mountains. Trail numbers correspond to hikes described in the chapter "Hikes"

HIKES

HALF-DAY AND DAY HIKES

1. Suðurnámur Mount Hike

Landmannalaugar Campsite – *Suðurnámur* Mount – *Vondugil* Valley – *Laugahraun* Lava Field ("*Laugavegur* trail") - *Landmannalaugar* Campsite

Loop hike
total distance: ~9 km (map), ~10-11 km (walking)
hike duration: 4-5 hours
elevation (min-max): 580 – 920 m a.s.l.
elevation gain: ~ 470 m
difficulty: easy to moderate

Suðurnámur **Mount Hike** is an easy-to-moderate half-day circular hike to the 200,000 years old mount's top for anyone who can conquer rather steep ascent and descent. Once you are on the summit, it offers you one of the best panoramic views in the area to North (*Frostastaðavatn* volcanic lake) and South (*Vondugil* Valley, *Laugahraun* Lava Field, *Brennisteinsalda* colorful volcano (881 m a.s.l.), *Bláhnúkur* mount (945 m a.s.l.), *Norðurbarmur* (757 m a.s.l.)). The hike along the *Suðurnámur* mount ridge is quite long, ~3 km, where you are perfectly exposed to all Highland's winds, though, be prepared for very powerful and chilly gusts; I would recommend to have an emergency 4th-layer for your outfit in the backpack, and hiking poles at steep slopes could be very useful.

The trail starts at the **road F224** [🌐 63.99837, -19.05120], its left side, just in front of a lava field, ~600 m from the parking lot and a fording river stream, or ~1.2 km from the campsite, there is a clear signpost showing the trailhead. Once you are at the trail, you quickly begin to ascend quite a steep slope, from 600 m to 747 m a.s.l., climbing for about ~700 m (if you hike the trail clockwise, this portion will be the hardest and less safe; - ascending steeper slopes easier and safer than descending them). Then you walk a bit down for 300 m and start to climb again the mount for ~ 1 km, from 700 m to 860 m a.s.l., and after that, there will be last 3rd main and tallest mount's peak *Suðurnámur*, which you have to climb from 860 m to 920 m a.s.l. through mostly gravel and rock. Descending will be rather quick, through a stony zig-zag trail, ~ 1 km, till a crossroad with a few other trails [🌐 63.99753, -19.11657] and an unnamed waterfall nearby, and then additional ~700 m down to the *Vondugil* valley with many water streams. Once you are in the vast valley (~630-620 m a.s.l.), your next task will be to safely ford many small and big streams. The amount of water in the valley will vary from season to season, depending on how snowy the preceding Winter was, and how warm the current Summer is, resulting in water volume from melted snow coming down to valleys. There are no bridges here, neither visible and well-marked trails (at least I did not see them in 2018), you have to find your way where to cross streams is the best for you; some, you can jump over with help of your hiking poles or big rocks, but others, you need to ford by taking off your shoes, although there aren't deep and fast streams, though, fording is easy and safe, only water is always super-cold. Usually, hikers ford streams either more to the left side of the valley, or to the right one. A wise practice is **to learn first from others**; you can watch for a while from the hilltop, how other hikers do, and then decide where would be the best to go for you. Either way, it will be only ~300-400 m flooded with streams, then an additional ~1 km hike through a muddy grassland till you reach the *Laugahraun* lava field with a good hiking trail like a highway, leading to the campsite (~1.5 km).

2. Laugahraun Lava Field Hike

Landmannalaugar Campsite – *Laugahraun* Lava Field ("*Laugavegur* trail") - *Vondugil* Valley – *Brennisteinsalda* Volcano Hot Springs – *Laugahraun* Lava Field near *Bláhnúkur* Mount – *Landmannalaugar* Campsite

Loop hike
total distance: ~4.5 km (map), ~5 km (walking)
hike duration: ~1.5-2 hours
elevation (min-max): 580 – 710 m a.s.l.
elevation gain: ~ 140 m
difficulty: easy

Laugahraun **Lava Field** is an easy "warm-up" circular hike for the beginning or if you are short in time. You can do it as a loop hike going around the entire lava field in either direction, alternatively, if there are elderly people with you or somebody who is not really prepared for hiking, you can use this trail as linear, and hike only to 1) *Vondugil* Valley (1.5 km, very easy trail) or 2) the *Brennisteinsalda* Volcano Hot Springs (2.5 km, last part is uphill and rocky) and

back. The most difficult portion of the whole trail is after smoky hot springs [🌐 63.99753, -19.11657] (if you hike it counter-clockwise), when you turn left; there will be for about 2 km (till the campsite) a lava field trail going along a water stream and the *Bláhnúkur* Mount at your right side. While the main trail is well marked, it has many trodden branches, sometimes confusing or misleading. Here, the trail is very rocky with many sharp like a blade lava stones, deep cracks and holes and it is progressing through a hilly terrain. I would suggest using at this place hiking poles, they will give you more fidelity during tricky maneuvers around lava rocks and cracks.

3. Bláhnúkur Mount Hike

Landmannalaugar Campsite – *Bláhnúkur* Mount – *Laugahraun* Lava Field – *Landmannalaugar* Campsite

Loop hike
total distance: ~6.5 km (map), ~7.5 km (walking)
hike duration: ~3-4 hours
elevation (min-max): 580 – 945 m a.s.l.
elevation gain: ~ 457 m
difficulty: moderate

Bláhnúkur **Mount Hike** is a "must" circular hike for experienced hikers to the summit of 60,000 years old bluish-greenish mount. You will get to the highest point in the area with magnificent panoramic view over almost 1/4 of the nature reserve *Friðland að Fjallabaki*, there will be a few higher mounts (> 1000 m a.s.l.) than the *Bláhnúkur*, but much farther to South, West and East. The trail starts 600 m from the campsite, near the *Bláhnúkur*'s mount slope, just after you cross a river by a small wooden bridge [63.98490, -19.05919], then you have a long narrow hiking trail up for ~1.5 km to the mount's summit (945 m a.s.l.). The ascending is not extremely steep, and the trail is well trodden and maintained with a few viewpoints, however, the trail is rather narrow, yet it allows you to pass by safely with descending people, although, it is better to do it at natural viewpoint "platforms", where many people can stand at the same altitude. This mount slope usually is the busiest among others; travelers who come to *Landmannalaugar* with tour buses just for a few hours do short hikes here to the summit and back for photography. After you pass the mount's peak (quite flat and wide), it will be a long descending (~1.8 km) slope trail with lose stones into a reddish ravine with a water stream at its bottom, which you have to ford (usually, there are stones available, no need for wet feet). Then, it will be just ~0.5 km to the *Laugahraun* lava field, very close uphill to *Brennisteinsalda* volcano hot springs (left trail), and ~2 km through the lava field to the campsite by using the same trail (right trail) as the *Laugahraun* lava field hike (see Hike #2).

4. Brennisteinsalda Mount Hike

Landmannalaugar Campsite – *Laugahraun* Lava Field – *Vondugil* Valley – *Brennsteinsalda* Volcano Hot Springs – *Brennisteinsalda* colorful mount/volcano – *Vondugil* Valley - *Landmannalaugar* Campsite

Loop hike

total distance: ~7.5 km (map), ~8.5 km (walking)
hike duration: ~3-4 hours
elevation (min-max): 580 – 881 m a.s.l.
elevation gain: ~ 321 m
difficulty: moderate

Brennisteinsalda **Mount Hike** is a relatively easy circular/linear hike for any level hikers, although, there are a few patches, where you have to be rather fit and have at least minimum experience in mountaineering (hiking poles advisable). You can do this hike either in the linear mode – by reaching the most colorful summit in the region *Brennisteinsalda* ("Sulfur Wave", *ISL*) and coming back with the same trail (linear trek: total trail distance with return ~7 km), or you can challenge yourself with more adventurous slightly longer circular trail (circular trek: total trail distance ~7.5 km) – walking through the whole mountain ridge and then descending to the *Vondugil* Valley, and finally to the *Laugahraun* lava field and the campsite.

The trail stars at the camping site, then you hike to the *Vondugil* Valley through the *Laugahraun* lava field (~1.5 km, very easy trail, almost a highway, see hike #2), then you turn left to the *Brennisteinsalda* volcano hot springs (~1 km, last part is uphill and rocky). At the smoky hot spring (690 m a.s.l.) [🌐 63.98187, -19.08836], you continue climb uphill through very rocky terrain (~300 m) to a popular viewpoint (~750 m a.s.l.) [🌐 63.98043, -19.09005], many hikers spend here at least 15 min or more to enjoy the surrounded views and a windless area. After the viewpoint, you have to continue the trail along the mount slope for ~300 m till you reach a fork-point [🌐 63.97917, -19.09525] and take a right trail (the left one is *Laugavegur* trail heading to *Þórsmörk*, see "Multiday Trekking" chapter), leading you (~400 m steep uphill, slippery gravel, lose rock) to the mount summit (881 m a.s.l.) [🌐 63.98093, -19.09559], which you'll find quite flat and wide, but extremely windy. During your ascending, at your right side [🌐 63.981275, -19.091752], there will be an unusual and awkward in shape rock formation (~12-15 m high), resembling an erected phallus with testicles (nature sometimes can work as an unbeatable artist with good sense of humor). If you've decided to make a circular trail, once you reached the *Brennisteinsalda* Volcano's summit, you take a descending trail at your left, walking at first Westwardly and then mostly to North along the mount ridge for about ~1.65 km (descent from 881 m to 620 m a.s.l.) till you reach a fork-point in the *Vondugil* Valley [🌐 63.99059, -19.09939], where you have to take the right trail, heading towards the *Laugahraun* lava field and then to the campsite.

5. Frostastaðavatn Lake Hike

Landmannalaugar Campsite – *Suðurnámur* Mount – *Frostastaðavatn* Lake – *Stútur* crater – *Landmannalaugar* Campsite

Loop hike
total distance: ~6.7 km (map), ~7.5 (walking)
hike duration: ~2-3 hours
elevation (min-max): 580 – 690 m a.s.l. + 33 m *Stútur* crater
elevation gain: ~ 110 m + 33 m
difficulty: easy

Frostastaðavatn **Lake Hike** is my favorite circular short-distance hike, which is easy to do, yet, it offers you most rich variety of different landscapes to explore, like a truly highland's lake *Frostastaðavatn* with turquoise water, surrounded by rhyolite volcanic mounts, mossed huge lava fields, patches of lava invaded water and reddish-pinkish craters like *Stútur*. This is a trail number one for landscape photographers; myself, I spent here a full day making tones of stunning unearthly beautiful panoramic images.

The trail starts at the campsite and you have to follow firstly the road **F224** for ~1.3 km to the massive lava field at both sides of the road, where the trail begins [🌐 64.00109, -19.04962]; there is a signpost pointing to the trailhead. Then, you have to climb up a not-very-steep slope for ~1 km to the mount top (670 m a.s.l.), where the view will be astonishing, in front of you the lake, at your left colorful volcanoes and lava flow invading the lake, and at your right, *Stútur* – the reddish cone-like picturesque crater. After the mount top, it will be easy descent for ~700 m to a nice viewpoint (with a parking lot) [🌐 64.01315, -19.04588]. At this point, you head back, you walk for ~500 m to the crater *Stútur* [🌐 64.01314, -19.04068] by **road 208**, then, if you wish you can climb on the crater's top rim and make a full circle hike (~33 m high, ~100 m in diameter); just be careful, the crater slope is rather steep, but there are steps and ropes, yet, it could be very slippery, especially after rain, make sure you take a good trail up, there are a few, and some can be closed due to danger of gravel/soil slides or damage made to vegetation and rock. After the crater, you walk for ~2.3 km to the beginning of the trail by roads **208** and then **F224**, and then back to the campsite.

6. Stútur Crater Hike

Landmannalaugar Campsite – *Stútur* crater – *Landmannalaugar* Campsite

Linear hike
total distance: ~6.5 km (map), ~7-7.5 (walking)

hike duration: ~2-3 hours
elevation (min-max): 580 – 590 m a.s.l. + crater 623 m a.s.l.
elevation gain: ~ 10 + 33 m
difficulty: easy

Stútur **Crater Hike** is the easiest and shortest hike you can make here to warmup yourself before more serious ones, yet, it can offer you plenty of exciting experiences about the region – you will see and climb on the top the most picturesque classical cone-like crater with reddish-pinky slopes surrounded by lava field covered with very old light-greenish moss. The trail starts at the campsite and you have to follow first the road **F224** for ~1.2 km to the massive lava field called *Námshraun* at both sides of the road, and then, after ~1 km walking, at the crossroad [🌍 64.00481, -19.03618], you turn left to **208 road**, which will lead you to the *Stútur* (additional ~1 km) [🌍 64.01314, -19.04068]. If you wish you can walk at the crater's rim and make a full circle hike around it (623 m a.s.l., ~33 m high, ~100 m in diameter); just be careful, the crater slope is rather steep, but there are steps and ropes, yet, it could be very slippery, especially after rain, make sure you take a good trail up, there are a few, and some can be closed due to danger of gravel/soil slides or damage made to vegetation and rock. After the crater, you can explore the area around, it has many well-trodden trails in the lava field called *Norðurnámshraun*, just be careful not to damage very old moss here, do not make new trails. You can also visit the *Frostastaðavatn* lake with turquoise water and invaded *Námshraun* lava in it (see previous hike #5), it is just over the corner (~400 m) with a nice viewpoint [🌍 64.01315, -19.04588]. To walk back, use the same roads **208** and **F224**, it is just ~3.2 km from the crater and ~3.6 km from the lake to the campsite.

7. Norðurnámur Mount Hike

Landmannalaugar Campsite – *Suðurnámur* Mount – *Frostastaðavatn* Lake – *Stútur* crater – *Norðurnámur* Mount – *Landmannalaugar* Campsite

Linear hike
total distance: ~11-12 km (map), ~12-13 (walking)
hike duration: ~4-5 hours
elevation (min-max): 580 – 792 m a.s.l.
elevation gain: ~ 212 m
difficulty: easy-to-moderate

Norðurnámur **Mount Hike** is an easy-to-moderate hike, which is combined with the *Stútur* hike (see previous hike #6). After visiting the reddish crater *Stútur* [

[⊕ 64.01314, -19.04068], you continue hiking uphill by either of two ridges (they look like rims of a bigger crater, and *Stútur* is situated just in its center), which surround the crater, to the top of the mount (792 m a.s.l.). You can start the hike at either of 2x trailheads, one is very close to the crater [⊕ 64.01370, -19.04305], the other begins at the junction of roads **F224** and **208** [⊕ 64.00503, -19.03618]. The first trail is ~2 km from **208** to the mount top, the second ~2.5 km (from the **F224/208** junction). After you have enjoyed for a while magnificent views from the mount's summit (you can see 2x beautiful lakes around, *Frostastaðavatn* at West, and *Ljotipollur* at North-East), you can return back by using the same or the second trail, or alternatively, you can descend the mount through its Northern hillslope [⊕ 64.02516, -19.01210], the trail is rather steep, but short (~600 m), once you descended, you can turn right and go back by the Eastern mount side along the lava field, it will be ~4 km to the **F224/208** junction. If you have time, you can visit as well a very deep volcanic lake *Ljotipollur* (see next hike #8) [⊕ 64.02969, -19.00663], it is only ~600 m North-East from the point [⊕ 64.02516, -19.01210] where you descended from *Norðurnámur*.

8. Ljótipollur Lake Hike
Landmannalaugar Campsite – *Suðurnámur* Mount – *Frostastaðavatn* Lake – *Stútur* crater – *Norðurnámur* Mount – *Ljótipollur* Lake – *Landmannalaugar* Campsite

Linear hike
total distance: ~13 km (map), ~14 (walking) + 4 km (around the lake)
hike duration: ~3-4 hours + 1.5 hr (around the lake)
elevation (min-max): 580 – 792 m a.s.l. (if you climb the *Norðurnámur* mount)
elevation gain: ~ 212 m
difficulty: easy-to-moderate

Ljotipollur **lake Hike** is, in my opinion, one of the best half-day hikes in the *Landmannalaugar* region, since it offers you many wonderful sights to explore. You can combine this hike with *Frostastaðavatn* lake hike (#5), *Stútur* crater hike (#6) and *Norðurnámur* mount hike (#7). *Ljotipollur* lake is a volcanic crater lake, which is amusingly named by Icelanders as an *"Ugly Puddle"* (*ISL*), despite the fact that it is actually very beautiful and rather big, a lake-size "puddle" (~1300 x 500 m). If you wish, you can hike around the lake, it is a good and not-too-strenuous hike, although terrain is quite rough and hilly; to make a full circle, it is ~4 km, ~1.5 hr walk. The crater in which the lake is situated [🌐 64.03514, -18.99838] has reddish-pinky-black-green very steep slopes (Western side: 60 m deep, 640 m – 580 m a.s.l.; Eastern side: 130 m deep, 710 – 580 m a.s.l.) formed by a huge volcanic eruption. This crater is a part of the *Veiðavötn* volcanic system, situated at North-East from the *Landmannalaugar* region. There is also a dirt road called *Ljótpollur*, which connects the lake and the **road 208**; - instead of hiking, you can visit the lake with your car.

9. Full Circuit Hike

Landmannalaugar Campsite – *Suðurnámur* Mount – *Brennisteinsalda* colorful mount/volcano – *Brennsteinsalda* Volcano Hot Springs – *Laugahraun* Lava Field *Bláhnúkur* Mount – *Landmannalaugar* Campsite

Loop hike
total distance: ~14 km (map), ~15-16 km (walking)
hike duration: ~5-6 hours
elevation (min-max): 580 – 945 m a.s.l.
elevation gain: ~ 1050 m
difficulty: moderate-challenging

Full Circuit **Hike** is a challenging hike for those who can stay only one full day in *Landmannalaugar*, but would like to see as much as possible. If you are enough fit, you need at least 5-6 hours to complete this hike, but in reality, with rivers crossing, over lava fields maneuvering, 6x steep mount slopes conquering, plus, you have to reserve a lot of time for photography, - your hike will have all chances to be transformed into a full-day hike (7-8 hours). Also, please, note, if you wish to see *Frostastaðavatn* lake (hike #5) and *Stútur* crater (hike #6), you need to add ~5 km to your full circuit hike distance, ~2 hr walk. You can do this loop hike in any direction, clockwise or counterclockwise, I do not see/know any preferences. Of course, by whatever reason, you can skip one mount from the three, making any combinations from the two left: *Suðurnámur* + *Brennisteinsalda*, *Bláhnúkur* + *Brennisteinsalda* or *Suðurnámur* + *Bláhnúkur*, - they are all interconnected.

11. Skalli Mount Mega Hike

Landmannalaugar Campsite – *Skalli* Mount – *Laugavegur* trail – *Brennisteinsalda* Mount – *Laugahraun* Lava Field – *Landmannalaugar* Campsite

Loop hike
total distance: ~16 km (map), ~17-18 km (walking) through *Laugavegur* trail
total distance: ~14 km (map), ~15-16 km (walking) through *Bláhnúkur* trail
hike duration: ~6-7 hours

elevation (min-max): 580 – 960 m a.s.l.
elevation gain: ~ 678 m
difficulty: moderate-challenging (weather-dependent)

Skalli **Mount Mega Hike** is a perfect full day-hike for those who love less-crowded, long and challenging trails. However, it is more weather/season dependent than the other local trails. I would recommend taking this trail through July to August (early September might be an option too), but not in June, since it well may be that the trail won't be visible/walkable due to thick layer of yet unmelted snow around *Skalli* Mount. To avoid any surprises, please, before challenging yourself to this trail, consult with local authorities (rangers, campsite ticket office staff) about the conditions the trail might be in (it can be even closed due to mud or thick layer of snow). The trail begins at the camping site, heading straight towards South, and then South-East following blue markers, through a short valley, leaving at your right side *Laugahraun* Lava Field and then *Bláhnúkur* Mount, and at your left side many water streams and tall mounts called *Reykjakollur* (~741 m a.s.l.) and *Norðurbarmur/Barmur* (~757 m a.s.l.) (the edge of gigantic volcanic caldera). After you crossed the last water stream in the valley [⊕ 63.97761, -19.04480], you start ascending a mountain ridge (from ~620 m to ~770 m a.s.l. and then to 820 m a.s.l.) walking for about ~2 km till you begin descending to the altitude ~780 m a.s.l. [⊕ 63.95880, -19.03088], right in the front of *Skalli* Mount (1027 m a.s.l.) [⊕ 63.95305, -19.04280], which you have to hike around (~1.5 km) from its East to South sides, climbing not more than 960 m a.s.l. [⊕ 63.95153, -19.04021], yet there will be very steep slopes and most probably snow patches. From here in a clear day you should be able to see a *Torfajökull* glacier at South. After you left *Skalli* Mount, there will be a plateau ~1 km and then again, a short climb (990 m a.s.l.) and descent (~1 km), a second plateau (~1 km), till you reach a fork trail point [⊕ 63.95821, -19.08490]: the right trail (~2.5 km) will head towards North and the *Bláhnúkur* Mount, plus, additional ~3.5 km to the campsite; the left trail will lead Eastwardly (~2 km) till a junction [⊕ 63.96411, -19.11717] with the famous and crowded *Laugavegur* trail and then ~2 km Northwardly to the *Brennisteinsalda* colorful mount, and additional ~3 km to the campsite. *Skalli* mount mega hike, if it is not too snowy and muddy, is very popular for mountain bike cycling, though, you have to watch your back.

12. Háalda Mount Storihver Hot Springs Mega Hike

Landmannalaugar Campsite – *Laugahraun* Lava Field – *Vondugil* Valley – *Háalda* Mount - *Storihver* Hot Springs – *Laugavegur* trail – *Brennisteinsalda* Mount – *Laugahraun* Lava Field – *Landmannalaugar* Campsite

Loop hike
total distance: ~21 km (map), ~22-23 km (walking)
hike duration: ~7-9 hours
elevation (min-max): 580 – 1128 m a.s.l.
elevation gain: ~ 568 m
difficulty: moderate-challenging (weather-dependent)

Háalda **Mount** *Storihver* **Hot Springs Mega Hike** is really a mega hike, in terms of altitude (*Háalda* Mount ["*high smooth mountain*", *ISL*] is really the highest in the region, 1128 m a.s.l.) and hiking distance (~21 km), and can be suggested only to well experienced mountaineers, enough fit and prepared hikers. The *Háalda* Mount is not only the tallest in the area, but also highly ranked in the local beauty competition; it is rhyolite brown-red-golden in colors, and it represents a North-West edge (rim) of the gigantic volcanic caldera of a complex volcanic system beneath of the *Torfajökull* glacier. From the *Háalda* summit you can observe spectacular panoramic views over almost the whole **Fjallabaki** **Nature Reserve**, including a hidden truly Highlanders lake (located at altitude 800 m a.s.l.) at the North-West foot of the mount called *Höfðavatn* (size 500x700 m). The trail starts as usual at the campsite and follows the famous *Laugavegur* trail through *Laugahraun* lava field, then meadow and cotton grass *Vondugil* Valley with water streams, up to an unnamed beautiful waterfall near a golden in color hillslope, where you have to ascend uphill (~630 -> 760 m a.s.l.) till you reach a fork point for many trails [🌐 63.99748, -19.11659]: the right trail is the part of *Suðurnámur* mount hike (see hike #1), the left trail is where you have to head for ~200 m and turn sharp left [🌐 63.99853, -19.11680], towards *Háalda* mount long ridge. It is ~5.5 km you made to the fork point from the campsite, and it is ~3 km left to the top *Háalda* summit (elevation gain: ~760 –> 990 m a.s.l. and then to the peak ~1128 m a.s.l.). Both ways up and down are quite steep, especially the descent, you go from 1128 m a.s.l. to a valley (900 m a.s.l.) just with a ~1 km descent trail. Once you are in the valley, there will be a vast plateau with not tall hills, you have to traverse it in South, South-East direction for about 4 km till you find a creek [🌐 63.95692, -19.15797], where you have to turn left and walk for another ~1 km along the stream Eastwardly, till you reach a place with geothermal activity called *Storihver* [🌐 63.95621, -19.14201]. From here it will be only ~4 km left hiking North-East by the famous *Laugavegur* trail (see chapter "Multiday trekking") to *Brennisteinsalda* mount, ~3 km to the campsite.

Figure 8 Panoramic view over Landmannalaugar Hut/Campsite (image #1,3) and a signpost for Laugavegur multiday trek (image #2)

Figure 9 Panoramic views over around Frostastaðavatn Lake (images #1, #2), a trail through Laugahraun lava field near the campsite towards Brennisteinsalda Mount (image #3), at the top of Suðurnámur Mount (image #4)

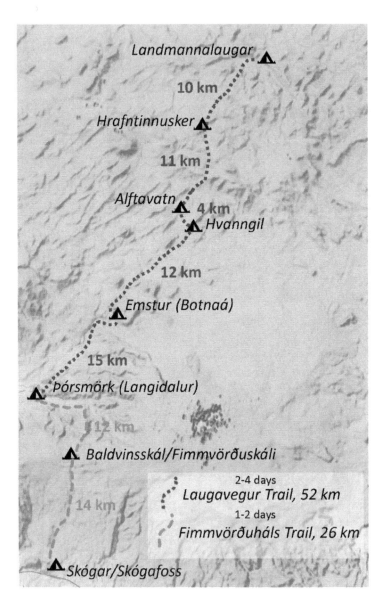

Figure 10 *Multiday Trekking, Laugavegur Trail (52 km) and Fimmvörðuháls Trail (26 km)*

MULTIDAY TREKKING

1. Laugavegur Trail
Landmannalaugar – Hrafntinnusker – Alftavatn/Hvanngil – Emstur (Botnaá) – Þórsmörk (Langidalur/Skagfjörðsskáli)

Linear trek
total distance: ~52 km (map), ~55-57 (walking)
hike duration: ~4 days (but also can be done in 2 days)
elevation (min-max): 220 – 1059 m a.s.l.
elevation gain: ~ 1700-1800 m
difficulty: moderate-challenging (weather-dependent)

Accommodation itinerary

d1 – *Landmannalaugar –> Hrafntinnusker*: 10 km (map), ~11-12 km (walking), 4-5 h

Landmannalaugar Hut/Campsite [🌍 63.99060, -19.06074] (9,500/2,000 *ISK*, 78 beds, WC, hot showers (500 *ISK*), kitchen, big dining place indoor and outdoor, 2x camping sites, small grocery shop + café in 2x school buses, free hot spring bathing nearby, open: ~Jun 25th – Sept 15th, it requires booking to stay in the hut at www.fi.is/en/mountain-huts/all-mountain-huts/landmannalaugar, no booking is needed for the camping site, payment with credit card or *ISK* cash, the place can be accessible with 4x4 jeeps by the roads Fjallabaksleið nyrðri (F208) or Dómadalsleið (F225)) -> *Hrafntinnusker* Hut/Campsite [🌍 63.93307, -19.16798] (9,500/2,000 ISK, 52 beds, kitchen, WC, no showers, gas, camping site, open: ~Jun 25th – Sept 16th, requires booking to stay in the hut at www.fi.is/en/mountain-huts/all-mountain-huts/hrafntinnusker, no booking is needed for the camping site, payment with credit card or *ISK* cash);

d2 – *Hrafntinnusker –> Alftavatn/Hvanngil*: 11/15 km (map), ~12/16 km (walking), 5-6 h walk

Hrafntinnusker Hut/Campsite (see above) -> *Alftavatn* Hut/Campsite [🌍 63.85760, -19.22684] (9,500/2,000 ISK, 72 beds, hot showers (~500 *ISK*), WC, gas, kitchen, dining room, big camping site, outdoor grill, open: ~Jun 25th – Sept 17th, requires booking to stay in the hut at www.fi.is/en/mountain-huts/all-mountain-huts/alftavatn, the place can be accessible with 4x4 jeeps by the road Fjallabaksleið syðri (F210));

Hrafntinnusker Hut/Campsite (see above) -> *Hvanngil* Hut/Campsite [⊕ 63.83180, -19.20570] (9,500/2,000 ISK, 60 beds, hot showers (~500 *ISK*), WC, gas, kitchen, dining room, 2x camping sites, outdoor grill, open: ~Jun 25th – Sept 17th, requires booking to stay in the hut at www.fi.is/en/mountain-huts/all-mountain-huts/hvanngil no booking is needed for the camping site, payment with credit card or *ISK* cash, the place can be accessible with 4x4 jeeps by the road Fjallabaksleið syðri (F210));

d3 – *Alftavatn/Hvanngil* –> *Emstur* (*Botnaá*): 16/12 km (map), ~17/13 km (walking), 6-7 h walk
Alftavatn/Hvanngil Hut/Campsite (see above) -> *Emstur* (*Botnaá*) Hut/Campsite
[⊕ 63.76581, -19.37390] (9,500/2,000 ISK, 60 beds, hot showers (~500 *ISK*), WC, gas, kitchen, dining room, small camping site, outdoor grill, open: ~Jun 25th – Sept 18th, requires booking to stay in the hut at www.fi.is/en/mountain-huts/all-mountain-huts/emstrur, no booking is needed for the camping site, payment with credit card or *ISK* cash, the place can be accessible with 4x4 jeeps by the road Emstruleið (F261));

d4 – *Emstur* (*Botnaá*) –> *Þórsmörk* (*Langidalur/Skagfjörðsskáli*): 15 km (map), ~16-17 km (walking), 6-7 h walk
Emstur (*Botnaá*) Hut/Campsite (see above) -> *Þórsmörk* (*Langidalur/Skagfjörðsskáli*) Hut/Campsite [⊕ 63.68489, -19.51271] (9,500/2,000 ISK, 75 beds, hot showers (~500 *ISK*), WC, gas, kitchen, dining room, small camping site, outdoor grill, open: May-Oct, requires booking to stay in the hut at www.fi.is/en/mountain-huts/all-mountain-huts/thorsmork-langidalur, no booking is needed for the camping site, payment with credit card or *ISK* cash, the place can be accessible with 4x4 jeeps by the road F249);

Trek itinerary

DAY 1. It starts at the *Landmannalaugar* Hut/Campsite [⊕ 63.99060, -19.06074] and follows the marked with red-white posts and then blue-white ones "*Laugavegur*" trail. This trail for the first ~3 km will be shared with other half-day trails, e.g. *Laugahraun* lava field hike (hike #2) or *Brennisteinsalda* mount hike (hike #4). Once you leave behind the most colorful mount in the region *Brennisteinsalda* (~3 km from the campsite), there will be a much-less-crowded trek, going slightly down (~810 -> 780 m a.s.l.) and then uphill (780 -> 950 m a.s.l.) for ~ 4 km till you reach an area called *Storihver* (~900 m a.s.l.) [⊕ 63.95617, -19.14196] with high geothermal activity, hot springs, bubbling mud pools, even small geysers, steam vents and water streams. From here, it will be only 3 km left to the hut/camping at *Hrafntinnusker* (~1000 m a.s.l.) [🌍 63.93307, -19.16798], at first slowly going up (900 -> 1040 m a.s.l.) and then down (1040 -> 1000 m a.s.l.). By a map total trail distance will be ~10 km, however, your actual walking distance will be longer, in most guides they give 11-12 km. The hut/campsite's name is *Höskuldsskáli* and it is located between two mounts: Western one is called as the place *Hrafntinnusker* (1141 m a.s.l.) with a trail up (~2 km one-way) to the top and some caves and steamers, through its Northern slope, another is *Stöðull* (1132 m a.s.l.), located East from the camp, also with a trail up (~1 km one-way). Be aware that starting from the *Brennisteinsalda* mount, there might be quite big snow patches, even the whole plateau (~5 km) can be covered with thick layer of snow and ice (not easy to walk) and in lowlands some mud and dense fog. To conclude – earlier in Summer you hike here, more snow you should expect, only in late July – August this part of the trail can be snow free, although not complete. Hikers call this portion the hardest in the "*Laugavegur*" trail, - too many unpredictable elements of environment come together: snow, ice, strong wind, fog, deadly cold, mud... etc., though, be well prepared. Another warning I would like to make here is that you have to be extremely careful with snow bridges and snow caves, these many-tones natural engineering constructions can easy collapse; it once had happened to me, but it was luck that I've got stuck to my waist-high in snow, and did not fall deeper, to the water stream under the snow bridge; though, pay attention, a bridge may look like a solid and trustworthy path, but it is constantly melting from above and beneath, and any time can collapse.

DAY 2. Next day in the morning, you start your hike at the *Hrafntinnusker* hut/camping and head South towards either the *Alftavatn* hut/camping (11 km trail by a map, 12 km walk) or ~3.8-4 km farther to the *Hvanngil* hut/camping (15 km trail by a map, 16 km walk). On your way, there will be 2x unbridged river crossings (~20-50 cm deep, season/weather dependent); one is 5 km from *Hrafntinnusker* and more like a stream, it should be easy to cross without wet feet [🌍 63.89401, -19.16706], and the other is 7.6 km from *Hrafntinnusker* and more like a glacial river [🌍 63.88126, -19.19749], thus, wider and wilder, it even has a name *Grashagakvísl*, here, you have to take off your hiking boots, put on sandals/crocs, carefully traverse it at its widest/slowest section, helping yourself with hiking poles; and the third one is ~1 km before *Alftavatn* hut/camping [🌍 63.86463, -19.21994] has some wooden bridges. After ~5 km strolling through a valley from *Hrafntinnusker*, at your left side ~3 km distance you will see a tall mount called *Háskerðingur* (~1281 m a.s.l.) [🌍 63.89333, -19.12252] with a small glacier *Kaldaklofsjökul* around it and an eponymous mount (~1167 m a.s.l.)

[🌐 63.88657, -19.15364] (you can climb it, detour is ~1.3 km one-way), and farther 5 km East there will be a much bigger *Torfajökull* glacier hiding beneath an eponymous volcano [🌐 63.89652, -19.00713]. Once you are leveled with these 2 glaciers you start long (~6 km) descending (1000 m -> 530 m a.s.l.) (be careful, it is rather steep and challenging terrain), till you reach the campsite [🌐 63.85760, -19.22684] standing near the *Alftavatn* lake ("Swan Lake", *ISL*) and a highland's road **F210**. If the weather is good, you can have short evening's hikes around, to *Alftavatn* lake (~500 m), (size: 1.5 x 0.8 km), or to a second smaller lake *Torfavatn* [🌐 63.84649, -19.27211], South-Westly, ~3 km one-way by the *Alftavatn*'s Northern shore, or to the mounts around the camp to enjoy the panoramic views. Relatively recently (2016-2017), "**Volcano Huts**" (www.volcanohuts.com) has opened here a new service, they constructed a new small building with Restaurant, Bar and Shop (open daily 7 am – 11 pm) with hot meals: **Breakfast** (~2,500 *ISK*, eggs, bacon, beans, hash browns); **Lunch** (~2,500 *ISK*, Soup of the day, salad, coffee and cakes); **Dinner** (~3,500 *ISK*, Grilled lamb, pork or chicken with sweet potatoes, sauce and veggie options); **Bar** (cold beer, hot coffee, cakes, candy bars); **Lunch pack** (2,500 *ISK*, Sandwich, candy- or energy-bar, fruit, soft drink or juice). If you have decided to go to the next *Hvanngil* hut/camping [🌐 63.83180, -19.20570], it is additional ~3.8-4 km farther (see DAY3).

DAY 3. Next day your aim is to hike to the next hiking hub, *Emstur* (*Botnar*) hut/camping [🌐 63.76581, -19.37390] with ~ 16 km trail, 6-7 h walk, with many river crossings, including 2x unbridged ones. The first unbridged river will be shortly after you left *Alftavatn* hut/campsite, ~1.6 km, river's name is *Bratthálskvísl* [🌐 63.84844, -19.21515]; next one is ~5.3 km from *Alftavatn*, just ~1 km once you left *Hvanngil* hut/camping and crossed with a wooden bridge [🌐 63.82561, -19.21354] *Kaldaklofsvísl* river; this second unbridged river is wider/deeper and bears a name *Bláfjallakvísl* [🌐 63.82259, -19.21942]. In most cases, fording here rivers is safe and without troubles (except unpleasant icy cold water), you just follow general rules for unbridged river crossing in Iceland, which are: 1) choose a widest section of the river, where slowest current is expected; 2) avoid river sections where cars ford as it will be deeper there, with trickier river bed; 3) ford rivers upstream from where cars ford, water there will be cleaner, with more predictable river bed; 4) use hiking poles to keep balance; 5) use light sandals/crocs to protect your feet from sharp and slippery stones; 6) avoid places where water is swirling in circle as it will be deeper there, with stronger current and trickier river bed; 7) please, consider that in general, rivers are deeper and wilder after rains, could become even uncrossable after heavy rains/snowfall, and in afternoons, when more snow and ice is melted during warmth of the day, though, rivers are shallower in mornings (if there was no night rain). After you crossed *Bláfjallakvísl* river, there will be a long valley with volcanic black sand and green hills, and the trail will crisscross with a highland road **F210** time to time, though, do not get on wrong trek, and follow the trails markers, signs and stone cairns (old Icelandic traditional man-made stacks of stones used in Viking's time to navigate and mark lands). There will be more rivers to cross, ~3.5 km from *Bláfjallakvísl* river, there will be a river called *Innri*

Emstruá, but now with a bridge [🌍 63.80559, -19.27829], although, sometimes it gets overflow, so you have to find your way through shallow water. After this point, it will be only ~7 km left to the *Emstur* (*Botnar*). The trail goes farther South-Vest through sandy valley along 2x mounts called *Útigönguhöfðar* (~688

m a.s.l.) [🌍 63.79344, -19.31789], then, a taller one called *Hattfell* (~924 m

a.s.l.) [🌍 63.79128, -19.35374] at your right side grabbing your attention for next ~3 km, then the trail will turn left and downhill for ~600 m till you reach the camp. Near *Emstur* (*Botnar*) hut/camping, there is an interesting very deep (max

~200 m) and long canyon called *Markarfljótsgljúfur* [🌍 63.76637, -19.39627] with a powerful river *Markarfljót* at its bottom, and it is believed to be created ~2,000 years ago by gigantic flood coming from the volcano *Katla* nearby, hidden under *Mýrdalsjökull* glacier, the flood was a result of melted glacier during *Katla* eruption. There is a short detour (~2 km one-way) hiking trail to the canyon and

its viewpoint from *Emstur* (*Botnar*) hut/camping; the trail starts here [🌍

63.76709, -19.37667] and goes along its edge to the viewpoint [🌍 63.76111, -19.40037] and then returns to the starting point (circular trail) going around a hill.

DAY 4. The last stretch of the "*Laugavegur*" trail is going through a land of ravines, thousand small and big creeks, furious rivers, deep canyons; it is the land of water here and rich vegetation, and not surprisingly, since it is a glaciers kingdom, where water controls over soil and rocks. Two biggest glaciers in Iceland, *Myrdalsjökull* and *Eyjafjallajökull*, hiding most powerful and dangerous volcanoes under massive ice shield, *Katla* and *Eyjafjallajökull* (erupted in 2010) had been shaping these lands for millions of years. Your aim for this day is to hike to *Þórsmörk* (*Langidalur*/*Skagfjörðsskáli*), ~15 km, 6-7 h walk, with one unbridged river crossing, and many others by stones and bridges. You start the trail in *Botnaskáli* (*Emstur*) going through a ravine with a small creek named as the place *Botnaá*, then downhill to a gorgeous deep canyon with a river *Fremri-*

Emstruá and a narrow bridge over it [🌐 63.75370, -19.36175]. After the canyon you turn sharp right, Westwardly, along the riverside, towards the bigger canyon *Markarfljótsgljúfur*, which you saw just yesterday, going through a valley with a few creeks for ~2 km and then turning again sharp left, and walking along *Markarfljótsgljúfur* canyon and *Markarfljót* river for about 9 km till the unbridged river *Þröngá* you have to ford [🌐 63.70226, -19.49978]. It is just before your last ascent uphill (220 -> 310 m a.s.l.), going through small forestated hill sides and bushland, only ~3 km left to the *Þórsmörk* (*Langidalur*/*Skagfjörðsskáli*) hut/camping site [🌐 63.68489, -19.51271].

2. Fimmvörðuháls Trail
Þórsmörk (Langidalur/Skagfjörðsskáli)   –   Baldvinsskál/Fimmvörðuskáli   – Skógar/Skógafoss

Fimmvörðuháls trail ("Five Cairn Pass/Trail", *ISL*) is a logical continuation for the *Laugavegur* trail (see above), going from *Þórsmörk* to *Skógar*, and many hikers do as such, however, it can be done as an independent "short" hike in either direction, and such route is very popular among many mountaineers and nature lovers who lack enough time for long trekking from *Landmannalaugar*'s rainbow mountains.

Linear trek
total distance: ~26 km (map), ~27-28 km (walking)
hike duration: ~2 days (but also can be done in 1 day, you need at least 9-10 h, but it will be safer, if you do it with slower pace, 12-14 h hike)
elevation (min-max): 220 – 1128 m a.s.l.
elevation gain: ~ 1200 m
difficulty: moderate-challenging (weather-dependent)

Accommodation itinerary
d1 – *Þórsmörk* –> *Baldvinsskáli/Fimmvörðuskáli*: 14/12 km, 4-5 h walk

1. *Baldvinsskáli* Hut [🌐 63.61089, -19.44098] (9,000 *ISK*, 20 beds, WC (latrine), no showers (!!!), no running water (!!!), no camping allowed with tents (!!!), small kitchen, small dining place indoor, open: summer time, it requires booking to stay in the hut at www.fi.is/en/mountain-huts/all-mountain-huts/fimmvorduhals-baldvinsskali , payment with credit card or *ISK* cash, the place can be accessible with 4x4 jeeps. If you need to cancel your booking, here are the rules: cancelled 30 days or more before arrival 85% of the amount, cancelled 29 - 14 days before arrival 50% of the amount, cancelled 13 - 7 days before arrival 25% of

the amount, cancelled less than 7 days before arrival - no refund , FÍ reserves the right to refuse refund due to late or no arrival, bad weather or other external circumstances.

2. *Fimmvörðuskáli* Hut [🌍 63.62182, -19.45045] (9,000 *ISK*, 20 beds, WC (latrine), no showers (!!!), no running water (!!!), no camping allowed with tents (!!!), small kitchen, small dining place indoor, open: ~ June 17th to August 31st, requires booking to stay in the hut at **Útivist´s office** (Laugavegur 178, Reykjavík) or by tel. +354 562 1000, payment with credit card or *ISK* cash) (www.utivist.is/english/fimmvorduhals-hut). If you need to cancel your booking, here are the rules: if cancellation is received 7 days before your booking or earlier, all is refundable except deposit fee 1.000 *ISK*, none is refundable, if cancellation is received within a week before the booking.

It is hard to say whether *Fimmvörðuháls* trail is less or more popular than *Laugavegur* trail, perhaps, they both deserve highest ranks in hiking scoring among tourists and locals, however, *Fimmvörðuháls* trail is twice shorter and can be done in a single day, if weather allows, thus, it is more attractive for those who are not prepared (or no time) for long trekking, yet, it offers unforgettable experience, unearthly beautiful and different landscapes, and strong sense of adventure and wilderness. The trailheads (bidirectional: *Þórsmörk* -> *Skógar*, *Skógar* -> *Þórsmörk*) are well connected with *Reykjavik* by daily buses and both have a few options for accommodation, food supply and eating, plus, half-day hikes at the place. The *Fimmvörðuháls* trail goes between two glaciers, *Eyjafjallajökull* and *Mýrdalsjökull*, which hide beneath their ice shields two nasty volcanoes *Eyjafjallajökull* (erupted in 2010) and *Katla* (erupted in 1918, and probably, it might erupt in close future), respectively. There are 2x mountain huts on the top of the pass, one is owned by **Ferðafélag Íslands** (FÍ) (www.fi.is) and called *Baldvinsskáli* [🌍 63.61089, -19.44098], the other is managed by **Útivist** touring association (www.utivist.is) and called *Fimmvörðuskáli* [🌍 63.62182, -19.45045]. Please, note, that it is not allowed to camp with your tent by these two huts (at the *Laugavegur* trail you can do it at any hut); and the reason for that is weather conditions on the top of the pass (altitude >1000 m a.s.l., very close to the ocean – it brings humidity, and two enormous in size glaciers – it brings freezing cold), it might be extremely windy or foggy, and the top can be covered with thick layer of snow, even in Summer. Thus, if you do not like to stay overnight in the hut or you travel on budget, you have no option but to hike this trail (26 km) in one day, which was proven to be doable, although, not easy, - you need for that a full long day (~ at least 9-10 h), preferably with good weather, be in good fitness and have some experience in high altitude hiking, be not overloaded with your backpack weight (ideally, it should be not more than 10-15 kg). If you still aren't sure whether you can/should do it or not, please, consider alternative options as such: 1) to do it in a guided group (it will be easier to hike with an expert than alone, there are many tour agencies which offer such guided hikes, at least do it with somebody who did it already); 2) to do it only a half-way *Skógar -> pass top* and then to hike back by the same trail (the uphill trail from *Skógar* to the pass top is easier than at the opposite side, - the trail from *Þórsmörk -> pass top* is steeper, the terrain is more dangerous, tricky to traverse, with deep canyons, narrow trail paths, at some places people can even experience vertigo); 3) instead of hiking *Fimmvörðuháls* trail, go to *Þórsmörk* and do there short half-day hikes, - there are many trails of different complexity in the valley and hills around *Þórsmörk*, they are worth to explore and aren't less beautiful than others, and can make you busy and happy for a few unforgettable days.

Trek itinerary

The trail starts at *Langidalur/Skagfjörðsskáli* hut/camping site (the end of the *Laugavegur* trail) [63.68489, -19.51271] and goes South-East down to the valley *Strákagil* for ~1 km till you find a long bridge [63.68050, -19.49390] to cross a river called *Krossá*. Once you crossed the river, it will be less than 1 km left to another hut/camping in *Þórsmörk* called Básar (*Goðalandi*) [63.67710, -19.48150] (www.utivist.is/english/basar-hut, 7,600 *ISK*, 83 beds, kitchen, WC, hot showers (500 *ISK*), gas stove, electricity (500 *ISK*), grill, camping (2,000 *ISK*)) and a bus station nearby (buses from/to *Reykjavik*). After Básar (*Goðalandi*) a long (~3 km) ascent will begin along a river and a mountain ridge South-East, and then South for ~2 km till you reach a mount called *Heljarkambur* (~770 m a.s.l.) [63.64833, -19.43187]. From this point it will be only 2 km left to 2x newly formed reddish volcanoes/mounts/craters named after the sons of Thor, the Norse God of thunder – *Móði* (1130 m a.s.l.) [63.63913, -19.44608] and *Magní* (1165 m a.s.l.) [63.63724, -19.44405] (you can climb on its top), surrounded by a *Goðahraun* lava field, they appeared in 2010 during the famous *Eyjafjallajökull* volcano eruption. You still can fill here warms of the soil and see steams and can appreciate the power of nature – our shared only-home – the Earth. After these two new mounts there will be ~2.5 km left to the *Fimmvörðuskáli* Hut (1100 m a.s.l.) or ~3.2 km to the *Baldvinsskáli* Hut (900 m a.s.l.). These two huts were built at the top of the pass between two glaciers, and the whole plateau can be covered with massive snow patches and be windy as hell, even in midsummer, though, be prepared accordingly, - even if weather forecast for the hike day is good, it can turn up-side-down within an eyeblink, from a sunny warm day to a nightmare with blowing snow storm, fog with almost "0" visibility or heavy rain. There is a memorial for three people who died here in

1970 because of weather. But since then, hikers get in troubles all the time on this path, every season Jun-Sep, when the trail is open. Only in July 2019, there were at least 3 accidents reported in local news, when a rescue team was used. There was a hiker who had fallen onto a deep ledge due to heavy fog on the trail, injuring himself and jamming his foot between rocks, when he was walking through a *Goðahraun* lava field, though, - be extremely careful, watch your every step, there are some ropes attached to rocks to hold on at too steep slopes – use them, also use properly hiking gears (trustworthy hiking boots with good grip, hiking poles, light crampons (can be helpful to walk on ice and snow), a GPS navigator with a map of this trail, I would recommend free OsmAnd, or OsmAnd+ www.osmand.net with off-line Iceland map, it has the trail, the App can work on either Android or iOS gadgets, smartphones).

d2 – *Baldvinsskáli/Fimmvörðuskáli* -> *Skógafoss*: 12/14 km, 4-5 h walk

Trek itinerary
Once you passed *Baldvinsskáli* Hut, you start a long descent initially through a Moon-like landscape, to other side of the mountain and glacial ridge. There are two trails which go down, - one is more to West, and closer to the river *Skógá* with ~26 beautiful waterfalls and a deep canyon [63.61040, -19.45117]; the other goes in parallel at ~1 km distance from the first more to East [63.61062, -19.43157], till they meet together at the bridge through *Skógá* river [63.57704, -19.44669]; it will be ~4.5 km from *Baldvinsskáli* Hut to the bridge by walking the Eastern trail, or ~5.4 km by the Western trail. Once you passed the bridge, it will be a long trek (~8 km) downhill along the furious river with many waterfalls (**"Waterfalls Highway"**), cracks, canyons, wandering around sheep and hikers, through greenish hilly terrain, until you reach a metal viewing platform above the *Skógafoss* [63.53187, -19.51047] (see "*Skógafoss*" chapter) with a metal staircase going down (~60 m) to the valley. At the base of the waterfall, you will find a basic camping site, restaurants, hotels and hostel, cafeteria, canteen, small food shop and touristic gears shop, a bus stop, museums (please, read for more details the "*Skógafoss*" chapter).

ADDIONAL INFO

Fí rules for huts/campings

Ferðafélag Íslands (FÍ) (www.fi.is) is one of the oldest (since 1927) Icelandic Touring Associations, which develops and promotes tourism in the country. FÍ owns 16 mountain huts/campings in Iceland, 4 of them in *Laugavegur* trail, +1 in *Fimmvörðuháls* trail.

Fí hut rules

1. If the warden is available, please, confer with him/her regarding your booking, where to sleep and specific hut rules
2. Quiet hours are from midnight until seven the next morning
3. No shoes inside the hut. Please, leave your hiking boots in entrance hall
4. Smoking inside the huts is strictly forbidden at all times
5. Please, leave the cooking area clean and tidy
6. Add water to the big pot on the kitchen stove, if needed
7. When leaving, please, make sure the hut is clean and tidy
8. Remember to pay for the accommodation and facilities
9. Help to keep the environment clean by not leaving your trash behind
10. You are hiking in Iceland to experience nature. Remember: Clean environment = Beautiful nature!

Fí camping rules

1. Camping is possible by all huts.
2. You do not need to book camping in advance.
3. Please talk to the warden before you put up your tent.
4. Price per person per night is *ISK* 2,000.- paid on the spot upon arriving.
5. You can pay with credit card or *ISK* cash.
6. Campers cannot use the kitchen or other facilities in the huts.
7. Campers have access to the bathrooms and drinking water as well as outdoor tables and benches.
8. Showers are available for 500 *ISK* for 5 min.
9. No showers in *Hrafntinnusker* or *Baldvinsskali*.
10. Everyone must take their trash with them from *Hrafntinnusker*, *Emstrur* and *Baldvinsskali* to the next hut.
11. *Landmannalaugar*, *Emstrur* and *Thorsmörk* have common tents for campers to use for cooking or eating. Campers need to bring their own cooking gear.
12. Camping outside of designated camping areas is forbidden by law.

Fí refund policy for huts

Cancelled 30 days or more before arrival 85% of the amount
Cancelled 29 - 14 days before arrival 50% of the amount

Cancelled 13 - 7 days before arrival 25% of the amount
Cancelled less than 7 days before arrival - no refund

FÍ reserves the right to refuse refund due to late or no arrival, bad weather or other external circumstances. FÍ does not insure their guests or their luggage. Guests travel at their own risk. FÍ urges their guests to buy travel insurance.

FÍ food supply
Please, note that it is not possible to buy hot, ready-made meals in most of the Icelandic huts. Thus, you will need to bring and carry your own food when hiking in Iceland. The exception being the huts along the popular *Laugavegur* hiking trail. There all the huts sell some supplies, such as backpacking dried food (~2,500 ISK), soda (~400 ISK), red bull (~500 ISK), juice (~250 ISK), instant coffee (~100 ISK), Snickers, Mars, Twix (~350 ISK), Chocolate (~800 ISK), as well as stoves (~4,000 ISK) and gas (230 g, ~2,500 ISK). Only in *Langadal* in *Þórsmörk* is it possible to buy beer and wine.

Figure 11 *Panoramic views at Skógá river with 26 waterfalls (image #1), Skógáfoss waterfall, 60 m high (image #2) and good navigation in mountains is essential for survival (image #3)*

Figure 12 *Cheers, amazing ICELAND!!! :)*

Made in the USA
Columbia, SC
24 January 2025

52370913R00037